Real Stories.

SUCCESSFUL IN HIS EYES

33 INSPIRING STORIES

SUCCESSFUL IN HIS EYES

Cover & Interior Design: Ruth Hovsepian

You picked up this book for a reason.

Maybe you're tired of feeling like you don't measure up.

Maybe your work goes unseen, your sacrifices unnoticed, your faithfulness uncelebrated by the world.

This book is our gift to you.

Let it serve as a reminder that God sees you, He celebrates you, and you are already successful in the eyes that matter most.

1 Samuel 16:7 (ESV)

For the LORD sees not as man sees: man looks on the
outward appearance, but the LORD looks on the heart.

Contents

A Note From the Authors

THE DINNER PARTY WAS in full swing when she slipped into the room, clutching that alabaster jar against her chest. The religious leaders noticed her immediately, because a woman with her reputation shouldn't be here. She had no business interrupting their important gathering; she had no right to approach their honored guest.

But she didn't care about their whispers or their disapproving stares. She had one mission, one moment that mattered more than anything else. She knelt behind Jesus, broke open her most precious possession, and poured perfume over His head. The fragrance filled the entire room.

The disciples erupted. "What a waste! This could have been sold for a year's wages and given to the poor!" They calculated her sacrifice in dollars and cents, measuring her gift against their definition of practical success.

Jesus said, "Let her alone: why are you troubling her? She has done a good and beautiful thing for me. She has done what she could. And this story will be told for centuries in memory of her" (Mark 14:6, my paraphrase).

She did what she could.

How many times have you felt like that woman, criticized for being you, for the choices that don't make sense to others, for looking a certain way?

Maybe you've felt the weight of society's scorecard pressing down on your shoulders. Success means climbing the corporate ladder. Success means achieving more, earning more, being more visible, more influential, more everything.

But what if you've been measuring yourself against the wrong standard?

What if the very moments you feel most unsuccessful in the world's eyes are actually your greatest triumphs in God's heart?

The woman with the alabaster jar didn't receive a promotion or public recognition. She received something far more valuable. Jesus saw her heart, honored her sacrifice, and declared her story worthy to be told wherever the gospel is shared. She found success not in worldly achievement, but in simple obedience performed in pure love.

In the pages that follow, you'll discover stories from women just like you, women who have learned that external accomplishments or society's applause don't measure true success. These brave sisters share how they found freedom from the exhausting pursuit of worldly recognition and discovered the deep peace that comes from living for an audience of One.

You'll meet the mother who chose homeschooling over a promising career. The woman who left her country, her home, to care for her aging parents and discovered riches money can't buy. The women who felt less than, some who were stamped with the world's disapproval, but found God's unwavering approval, unconditional love, and His unshakeable faithfulness.

Each story reveals a different facet of what it means to be successful in His eyes. Sometimes it looks like staying when others go, sometimes it's going when others stay. Sometimes it's saying yes to the small and hidden, sometimes it's having the courage to step into the spotlight God provides.

But here's the beautiful truth threading through every testimony: Success in God's economy often appears as failure to the world's watching eyes. The last becomes first. The humble are exalted. The servant becomes great. The woman who pours out her treasure for love discovers she's gained everything that truly matters.

If you've been carrying the heavy burden of never measuring up, these stories will lift that weight from your weary shoulders. If you've wondered whether your ordinary days have any significance, these women will show you how they are very significant. If you've struggled to find your worth in a world that seems to value everything you're not, you'll discover the liberating truth of who you already are in Christ.

God values your patient endurance through seasons when you feel forgotten. He treasures your willingness to serve in ways that earn no earthly recognition. He celebrates every moment you choose His voice over the world's demands.

You don't have to earn His love or prove your worth through achievements. You're already successful in the eyes that matter most, not because of what you've done, but because of Whose you are.

Let these stories remind your heart of this truth: When you do what you can with a heart full of love, when you pour out your life as an offering of worship, when you choose faithfulness over recognition, you are living successfully in His eyes.

Be encouraged by women just like you, who have found their place as princesses in the kingdom of God. It is our prayer that you'll find your princess crown in these pages.

SUCCESSFUL IN HIS EYES

OBEDIENCE

Chapter 1

Where the King Reigns

"The best you can be is obedient." —Pastor Dennis Pearrow

I settled into my usual front row seat, savoring the warmth from my coffee mug and absently fidgeting with a highlighter and pen. Above me, fluorescent lights hummed as I opened my Bible and flipped to the completed workbook pages prepared with answers for today's discussion. But the facilitator caught me off guard when she bypassed the study guide and posed a question to the room: "Do you love God?"

"Why even bother asking that?" I thought, and opened my mouth with the only acceptable response, but nothing came out. My throat constricted as if someone had wrapped their fingers around it. Heat crept up my neck, and I shifted in my plastic chair, suddenly aware of every sound in the room. That simple yes refused to emerge. For the first time in my Christian life, I knew that to answer in the affirmative would be a lie, and God had decided I wouldn't be speaking it anymore.

"Love Him?" The question echoed in my head as I stared at my workbook, words blurring together and my pen shaking against trembling fingers. Class continued, my mind reverberated one thing: "I'm an imposter."

The drive home was just as uncomfortable. God invaded my thoughts with song lyrics that further incriminated me: "I love you, Lord, and I lift my voice."

"I know. I know," I confessed. "I sing all the worship songs, but I don't feel it. How am I supposed to make myself feel something I don't? I want to love you. But I can't manufacture it." Hysteria took over. "If I'm being completely honest (and apparently we're doing that now), I don't even *want* to love you. Because if I did, you'd probably make me move to some remote village where I'd starve, contract malaria, or end up as a midnight snack for an anaconda."

Silence.

Then, clear as day, I heard God's response. Not an audible one. Louder than that.

Are you done?

Now it was my turn to be silent.

Then, like Job, God confronted me with a hefty dose of reality. *You can't even take a meal to your neighbor without breaking out in a cold sweat. Do you think I'm ready to ship you off to represent Me in Africa? How about we start smaller? Slow your roll.*

I released the breath I'd been holding with a laugh at God meeting me in my mess with words I actually understood. I smiled, picturing Him chuckling, the way I did when my child would huff and stomp while learning to ride a bike. In that moment, I realized our Father cheers for us in the struggle as much as He does for our success. That gave me the confidence to relax my knuckles against the steering wheel and finally admit the truth: "I don't know how to love You, and I'm not convinced it would be in my best interest."

There it was. I feared that loving God would require too much of me, and I was right about the cost; I was just clueless about how much it would be worth it.

What happened next shattered my assumptions about how God operates. I braced for spiritual boot camp tactics designed to whip my rebellious heart into shape. Instead, my Father answered with conviction. I felt a gentle and insistent knock on my heart's door, prompting me to confess sin, not as punishment, but to lance the infection that was poisoning my soul. God had called me to women's ministry, and He knew that I had to battle for my own freedom before I could help others.

I had my marching orders, and I was willing, albeit grudgingly, because the assignment was terrifying. This was not a simple apology for an everyday slight, but a confession about things from my youth, dark chapters I'd buried so deep I'd almost convinced myself they weren't real. After being victimized in ways that left deep wounds, I made terrible choices in my brokenness. The things I had done, the ways I acted out my pain, haunted me with shame so thick I could barely breathe when I thought about them.

But God refused to let me hide any longer. Faces appeared in my mind of people who deserved to hear the truth from my lips. People who should know me intimately but didn't. People who'd felt me retreat without understanding why. People who deserved to know it wasn't because of them, but because of sin. My sin.

I felt like I had a dilemma, but a pastor I'm acquainted with in Oklahoma would say, "Christians don't have dilemmas, only opposition," and he'd be right. There was no dilemma, only opposition, even if that opposition was me.

I wish I could say I quickly obeyed. Instead, I panicked. "I don't want to do this. I can't. Why do I have to? I've already confessed, and You forgave me. What does this have to do with others?"

I issued complaints, and the Spirit countered: "Confess your sins to one another ... that you may be healed" (James 5:16 ESV). He made the case that when we're transparent with others, they're more willing to walk the road to freedom with a veteran by their side. Still, I argued. I resisted. I stalled. And my Father let me.

To be clear, I never screamed at heaven or shook my fist. Sure, I procrastinated. I lamented. I wallowed in a cycle of self-pity and anger. The same resentful script played over and over in my head. "If God is sovereign, He should never have let the abuse happen in the first place, then I wouldn't have done what I did. And if He hadn't let certain people hurt me, then I wouldn't have to deal with this now." I have a great imagination and excel at blaming others. So I did, and my Father listened.

As my Creator and Judge, He could have responded to my dissent with harshness. Instead, He engaged me with the understanding of a Father who'd already experienced all of my grief and sorrows (Isaiah 53:3–4). He gave me time. He encouraged me through prayer, Scripture, and the same worship songs He'd used to convict me, yet He didn't relent or back off the charge. His gentle pressure on my weary soul carried the same message. "Keep attending your Bible studies and conferences. Keep writing and doing all the things. But I'm not moving another inch until you deal with this. I'll wait right here until you're ready. I'm not going any further."

The words echoed Moses' confrontation in Exodus 33, after Israel's betrayal with the golden calf, God drew a line. He'd send an angel before them, but His presence was off limits until they were willing to deal honestly and radically with their sin. The message was clear: They could have religion without relationship, or they could have both.

My choice mirrored theirs perfectly. I could maintain my spiritual routine and distance myself from God, or I could swallow my pride and step back into His presence; He wasn't going to pretend my disobedience didn't matter.

Overall, it took me about a month to comply, or rather, build up the courage, and another week to engage each person. Relief didn't flood through me afterward, though; instead, I felt like I'd stripped naked in a crowded room. My skin crawled with vulnerability. I felt exposed and in danger. When abuse victims excavate the wreckage of their trauma, they often feel victimized all over again. God knew this would hurt, and His heart broke over the necessity (John 11:1–44), though He refused to leave me buried. The choice was mine, but the terms were His.

Every conversation felt like free-falling from a cliff; I felt my stomach in my throat as I waited for impact. I'd light each confession like a match to dynamite, then squeeze my eyes shut, bracing for the explosion that would obliterate everything. But the blast never came. Instead, God's faithfulness caught me mid-fall, again and again. The disasters I'd scripted in sleepless nights remained fiction. No relationships shattered. No secrets weaponized against me. No devastating consequences materialized. Those catastrophic scenarios I'd played out in my mind were nothing but imagination fueled by faithlessness, prison bars I'd welded with my own anxious thoughts.

What appeared to be my undoing was, instead, my Father teaching me to do justice, love mercy, and walk humbly with Him (Micah 6:8).

The Beautiful Aftermath

Something shifted in my chest as I looked back over the wreckage I'd expected but never found. Gratitude washed over me, not the polite thank-you kind, but the breathless amazement of someone pulled from drowning. I hadn't navigated those conversations alone. When my voice failed, He provided what needed to be said. When I braced for chaos, peace settled around me like a blanket. The transformation was staggering; relationships I'd thought were terminal began breathing again. People who'd only known my carefully curated persona embraced the broken, real version without flinching.

But the most stunning change was what happened in my heart. Each time God caught me when I jumped, each moment His grace met my weakness, something I had been unable to force began blooming naturally—love, actual, authentic love for Him. The connection blindsided me; obedience had been the soil where affection took root.

As I practiced scary, pride-crushing obedience, God cultivated something beautiful. I fell in love with my Savior. His answer to my prayer didn't involve foreign missions (though that might have been easier). It was exactly what I needed. He used the back door of my stubborn heart, and while I focused on the hard work of confession and humility, He slipped in and did what I couldn't do for myself. Every revelation of His character, every proof of His faithfulness, had been wooing me into something real.

In humbling myself before others, I'd been learning to bow before my King.

I picture her now, that woman whose knuckles had gone white against tan leather, whose breath came in shallow bursts as she wrestled with a question that shattered her world. She'd been right to tremble; loving God would strip away every illusion of control. What she couldn't see was that, in protecting her wounds, she was cutting off circulation to what needed healing.

Kevin Shelton, a pastor back home in Tennessee, is fond of saying, "You only have to change one thing, and that's everything." He's not wrong. God might ask you to step toward the very thing that makes your pulse hammer in your throat. Be obedient, even when it burns. He's not trying to make your life harder. He's endeavoring to liberate and deploy you. Trust your Creator to know precisely how to cultivate what you cannot for yourself.

In God's economy, greatness is measured by our acceptance to move forward with His plan when everything in us wants to run in the opposite direction. Obedience opens the gateway to life as it was meant to be in His kingdom, both now and always. This kingdom becomes a present reality when we choose His way over our own. Here is what success looks like in God's kingdom: Obedience is equal to self-denial; self-denial for another's benefit is sacrificial love; sacrificial love puts the gospel on display; displaying the gospel is what it means to follow Christ (Matthew 16:24–28). As my pastor would say, "The kingdom of God is where the King reigns."

Jeremiah 31:3 (ESV)
I have loved you with an everlasting love;
therefore I have continued my faithfulness to you.

KIMBERLY PEARSON learned how to thrive when God confronted her self-righteous religious activities and exchanged them for a genuine relationship. Now, as a certified biblical counselor and Faith Bible Institute graduate, she guides Christian communicators through valuable introspection.

Kimberly creates intimate retreats for those who proclaim truth while carrying silent wounds that bleed into their ministry. Her approach strengthens the messengers by addressing trauma and examining theology. She helps women share their testimony fearlessly with integrity rather than being ruled by it. As a former police officer and current chaplain, she tackles difficult topics with sensitivity.

She is a contributing author to *The Advent Collection* (December 2025) and author of *No Longer Confused* (2026).

Connect with Kimberly on her websites at kimberlypearsonministries.com and womenspeakers.com.

Chapter 2

One Yes, One Step, One Treasure

Walking into the room bathed in beautiful sunlight, I remind myself to focus on the person I'm visiting, setting aside the long list of things I need to accomplish today. My heart swells with purpose as I approach my mom, Sarah, who is ninety-six and lives in a memory care facility. My simple yes to God today is to shower her with love. Thankfully, she still remembers me, and for that, I am deeply grateful.

As I pass others at different stages of memory loss, I pause to smile and greet them with a cheerful "Good morning!" They recognize me now, and it warms my heart as I head to my sweet mom's room.

As I enter, her face brightens with a smile. Our familiar routine is soothing; I help her settle into her blue glider, beneath a picture of Daddy. I curl her hair with the curling iron, one of her favorite activities. We talk and often go over the same stories she shares each visit. "You know your dad told me ... move to Bellevue Woods and you'll be safe there."

I smile. "Yes, Mom, you did so well, and I know he's proud of you." Time feels suspended for her. Dad has been gone nearly sixteen years, and it took her twelve years before we could help her decide to move. That day was difficult for all of us.

We reminisce about cooking, canning vegetables, and the laughter-filled moments around the table as she ironed my siblings' clothes and Dad's work shirts. I can still picture my brothers chasing her around the house, even sitting her on top of the refrigerator for some playful fun while Dad was at work. It's these little memories that bring joy to Mom and me.

As I finish styling her hair, I pause to apply lotion to her tiny arms and puffy ankles. I want her to feel cherished and to know love in every way I can give. Seeing the light return to her eyes and hearing her laughter when I say, "Let's take a picture," fills me with a sense of fulfillment, a kind of success. I know then that God is using me in her life. It's my yes.

Success is partly defined by achieving a desired outcome; however, from a biblical perspective, success mainly depends on faithfulness to God and aligning with His will. The core of a believer is this: knowing and doing the things, big or small, that honor God. Pretty simple, right? Well, not always. The world is shouting in your ear, "Do more," "Be more," "Push harder," or "You can certainly do better than this!"

The result is that we become frustrated and quickly want to give up because the struggle feels too hard. But as believers, when we are in the middle of big or even small difficulties, seeking Him will lead and guide us to do things that hold more value than earthly things. He will direct us to be His instruments of love, gentleness, compassion, and kindness. Sounds like a Scripture I love. "Therefore, as God's chosen people, holy and dearly loved, clothe yourselves with compassion, kindness, humility, gentleness, and patience" (Colossians 3:12 NIV).

I sometimes reflect on the women in the Bible and imagine how they felt within their world. I think about Mary, the young virgin chosen by God. To many, she was just an ordinary girl from a small town, but God's plan for her life changed everything. Was it easy for Mary to say yes, or was agreeing always expected? Did women even have the choice to refuse, or was saying no not an option at all? I imagine her lying in bed at night, realizing her belly is growing, and then feeling the baby move. Did she fearfully ask God, "Why me?" I wonder if she regretted her yes to Jehovah.

The angel Gabriel informed Mary that her relative Elizabeth was expecting a child. Even at an advanced age, Elizabeth—who believed she was barren—was probably surprised by her pregnancy. I wondered if she kept thinking, "No, this just can't be!" Any doubts Elizabeth might have had before Mary's arrival were quickly resolved by a joyful and beautiful moment. Luke 1:41 NIV describes it: "When Elizabeth heard Mary's greeting, the baby leaped in her womb, and Elizabeth was filled with the Holy Spirit."

Mary confidently trusted Jehovah's guidance. Her visit with Elizabeth, as recorded in Scripture, must have brought her pure joy. Throughout her life, she served as His vessel, and I can imagine it wasn't always easy or glamorous. How did she feel? Did she realize that God intricately designed her life, with each step part of His master plan? Her first reply to the angel was a simple, "Behold, your handmaiden ..."—her yes. She continued to say her yes every day. Following God's lead is true success! It's a moment-by-moment journey of spontaneity and surrender to His will.

As you reflect on Mary's life and your own, remember that success isn't measured by praise, followers, or even achievements, but by your willingness to say yes to God's plan. Mary's quiet yes gives us such courage as we serve the Lord in our world today.

Embrace the beauty of your journey, trusting that every step you take—big or small—is important in the eyes of the Lord. Your story, like Mary's, testifies to "God's in charge" moments. These moments show a success that comes from faith, love, and obedience. As Ecclesiastes 3:11 (NIV) reminds us, "He has made everything beautiful in its time."

After visiting Mom, I stepped outside to wait for my husband. Usually, he joins me, but today he had other plans. So, I decided to sit on a bench and review notes for an upcoming speaking engagement. As I held my notes, I saw an older man roll his wheelchair up next to me. Now, it was decision time. Should I smile, greet him, and then focus on my notes, or should I open my heart to what God might be doing? Could this be my yes? Oh my!

I chose to smile, and almost instinctively, I asked, "How is your day?"

His face lit up. "I'm okay." Our conversation seemed to flourish naturally. He opened up about his late wife, feelings of loneliness, health issues, and his son's fight with cancer. When he brought up cancer, I mentioned that I am a survivor of esophageal cancer. He said, "A friend of mine had that and didn't live very long."

I shared with him my promise to God—to tell others how He blessed me and healed me from cancer, and now I strive to honor that vow by sharing His faithfulness. I also shared with him how I had given my life to Christ at the age of nine.

As we talked, his eyes brightened, and he exclaimed, "You know what? I was saved at the age of twelve. What *joy*!" In that instant, we both felt the warmth of God's love, realizing how His divine timing brought us together.

My husband came to pick me up, and I felt like I was floating to the car, my heart overflowing with gratitude. It was my spontaneous yes. I knew I was right where God intended at the perfect time, following His direction. That's what I call success! It's about paying attention to God in the moment and trusting His guidance in our lives.

Years ago, I heard a beautiful story that reminds me that sometimes all we need to do is open our eyes to what God has already given us. The famous short story, "Acres of Diamonds," which is part of Russell Conwell's well-known lecture, tells the story of a wealthy Persian farmer, Ali Hafed, who sells his land to search the world for diamonds after hearing about their value, only to die in poverty. The man who later buys Ali's farm discovers the world's most magnificent diamond mine on the very same land, showing that Ali Hafed was unknowingly standing on his own riches. This story is an allegory that encourages people to recognize and develop the opportunities and resources already present in their own lives and environments.

You and I need to remember that true success in life comes from embracing God's plan. Just as Ali Hafed was unknowingly standing on a treasure, you are surrounded by blessings and opportunities that God has placed in your path. When you learn to say yes to God in the here and now, trusting His wisdom and seeing your life through His eyes, you unlock the riches of His grace and purpose. Let your heart be inspired to recognize that God's greatest treasures are often found within the steps you're taking today. Walk confidently in faith, knowing that with each yes to Him, you are stepping into the abundant life He has prepared for you. That is success in God's eyes.

My mom, in her own way, learned to say yes to God—right before my eyes! She was saved when I was a small child, and with five children, she showed God's love in all the ways a young mother would want. I should also mention that her life wasn't easy. Mom cooked, canned, did laundry, ironed, and loved on us kids. She was the only believer in our home at that time; it wasn't a perfect life.

As a young woman, a new believer, and a mother of five, she faced each challenge head-on. I now realize that my love for "style" came from my sweet Mom. She taught us to make the most of what we have by dressing our best. Every day, as my Dad's return from his mechanic job neared, she would freshen up. Many times, she would change into a pretty starched and ironed dress, adding just the right touch of rose-scented fragrance. In her own way, she was showing love to my dad by putting in extra effort to look pretty for him. This was her way of being a woman of God and teaching us kids; this was her yes to Jesus.

I learned from the best. Even though her yes was not always welcomed, she kept learning about God through Bible study, worship, and many prayers. God answered those specific prayers for my Dad's salvation many years later. God is faithful!

Walking in success is about growing in Christ and saying our own yes to what honors and glorifies Him—the small, the big, and the sometimes overwhelming or scary things that come to us. Serving Him by saying yes brings pure joy! But the "treasure" is knowing that in God's eyes, we have succeeded. Saying yes to Him—one yes at a time—is what Paul meant when he wrote in Colossians.

> Colossians 3:23 (NIV)
> Whatever you do, work at it with all
> your heart, as working for the Lord.

JUDY BONE is a vibrant speaker, author, and experienced Christian Image Consultant whose contagious joy brightens every room she enters. Her chapter, "One Yes, One Step, One Treasure," reflects her strong dedication to empowering women to embrace their God-given potential.

Judy authored an Amazon #2 bestseller, *In His Glow: Guiding You to God's Bright and Beautiful Path*. She highlights her talent for blending personal triumph with faith.

Her signature message, "Let's Get Glowing," resonates with women of all ages, encouraging them to embrace their natural beauty and cultivate confidence.

Besides writing, Judy is a guest on the radio, TV, and podcasts, sharing her uplifting stories. Through her ministry, she seeks to help women flourish, reminding them they are loved and capable of achieving everything God desires for them.

Connect with Judy on her website at judybone.com.

CHAPTER 3

No Difference Except Their Address

"NO." I'D SAID IT a dozen times. Maybe two dozen. My friend wanted me to go to the county jail for ministry, and I wanted nothing to do with it.

I wasn't interested. Honestly? I felt a little "better than" the people behind those bars. But God had other plans. Plans that would take me from no to yes, from county jails to maximum-security prisons, and change everything I thought I knew about His love.

It started with a friend who wouldn't take no for an answer. She hounded me for months to accompany her to the county jail for ministry. I said no countless times. But she was persistent. I finally told my friend I'd go once to get her off my back more than anything. That one time turned into over 150 times. Every Thursday night for three years, I walked through those county jail doors. Why? Because God showed up. I watched Him soften hardened hearts. I watched people change as they encountered His love for the first time. When I saw how God showed up, I knew I had to show up too.

It was uncomfortable at first, but we settled into a beautiful routine filled with Holy Spirit moments and massive amounts of grace. We watched God work and touch the lives of those we ministered to. We knew we were in the right place. The right place is a perfect place to be, until God has another place for us. A place that's even further out of our comfort zone. Sometimes, it's a place we'd never imagine we'd go.

I worked at a rural health clinic during the day, and a doctor there, aware of my jail ministry, wanted to introduce me to his patient, a woman who had a full-time prison ministry. She'd served time in prison herself and was now ministering to inmates like she had been.

Again, my immediate reaction was, no. I was perfectly happy ministering in the county jail. But the prison? That's for serious offenders, and it was a step in a direction I never wanted to walk toward. The doctor didn't have his listening ears on that day. He brought her to my office anyway and introduced us despite my hesitation.

That invitation led me, once again, in a direction I didn't want to go.

My husband and I pulled into the parking lot of the prison. Razor-sharp wire topped the fence surrounding us. I stepped out of the car, fearful, wondering what we'd gotten ourselves into. We walked through the first metal gate. It slammed behind us: metal on metal, echoing through my chest.

I thought, "I don't have the key to open that gate back up. I'm stuck."

Terror gripped me. My stomach twisted into knots. My knees knocked so loud they could be heard in the next county. We were headed into the prison.

The guard told us to remove all items from our pockets. Then she patted us down quickly, efficiently, and impersonally. She rattled off the dos and don'ts, as well as what to do if something happened inside.

Wait, what was going to happen, and why wasn't I told this before now?

The guard told us there was no talking aloud. No problem. I held my breath anyway.

Oh, if only I could be Spiderman, cling to that brick wall, and inch myself down this path, far away from that yellow line.

I prayed, "Lord, do you hear my plea? I could really use Your help right now."

How did I get here? And what was in store for me on the other side of these walls?

That initial trip into prison was nothing like what I had envisioned. Our first night? The men's unit. Before meeting the men, a volunteer handed us each a piece of cardboard. "Write your sins on one side," she said, "and on the other side, write how God redeemed you." They called it a cardboard confession.

I remember thinking how cool it was, but half joking, I told my husband not to write our nasty stuff. I mean, we were in prison, and I didn't want to get locked up. However, I decided to tell it all. My card told the truth: abuse, addiction, adultery, and my attempt to end it all. All the ugly. God had met me at my well of destruction and showed me another path, one where He would heal my broken heart and restore my faith in who I was and who He said I was. And now He was asking me to share His redemptive power and grace with these men.

We paraded around the prison with those signs, bearing all of our sins for everyone to see. As the inmates read our sins, from abuse to addiction and adultery, we turned the cards around so they could see what God had done for us, how He redeemed us. We showed them that we were no better than they were. We were simply saved by God's grace.

We moved into the chapel for the service. The guards required us women to sit separately from the men, so we sat in chairs on the stage while the male volunteers sat among the inmates. From my perch on that stage, I could see everything: the rows of plastic chairs, the concrete walls, the men filing in.

I was thankful for my seat on stage, not because it helped me feel safer, but because I could see all the men in the room—their eyes, their faces, and their sizes. They were large, strong men, many with tattoos covering parts of their bodies, some covering almost the entire body. To look at these men in any other situation would elicit fear and trigger the fight-or-flight response. But what I experienced was completely different.

God lent me His eyes that evening, and I saw them as little boys who were lost and hurting, craving something more. And in that moment, everything I thought I knew about "criminals" and "offenders" shattered.

We started the service with praise and worship. Surprisingly, the inmates themselves provided the music, voices raised in songs I recognized from my own church. Then the speaker delivered a message of redemption. It was real, raw, and touched the men in ways I hadn't imagined. Many of them broke down in tears, not the kind that just trickles down a cheek, but the kind that accompanies a heart full of repentance.

You see, these men knew the Bible. People preached to them almost every day of the week, but those messages carried religion and condemnation.

This was different. This was a time to feel the Holy Spirit's pure love. One of us had just shared the message of redemption, a self-confessed sinner who'd received God's redeeming grace. The truth is that we are all sinners, and I could see, for maybe the first time in my life, that these men, though they had committed serious acts of violence, were God's beloved too. He loved them just as much as He loved me. There was no difference except their address.

Most of them didn't resent being in prison. They knew they had a debt to pay for their actions. But that evening, they understood that there was One Who had paid their debt in exchange for their salvation. And they knew, they *knew*, the prayers of their mothers, aunts, or grandmothers had kept them alive to receive it. They were grateful with every fiber of their being. My bird's-eye view of that night changed me as much as it changed them. I could see them through the love and compassion of our Father's eyes, and I would never be the same.

The next evening, we ministered to the women. The transformation was equally as powerful as the night before. Again, I initially pictured these ladies with condemnation. They had done what they had done and were where they needed to be. But God softened my heart toward them and showed me that their mistakes were no different than the ones I'd made. The lies they had believed about themselves came from the same enemy. And God was going to bring forth new wine out of all of us. He was going to use His daughters on both sides of the prison wall to show the world what forgiveness looks like, what the love of our Father looks like when we feel unlovable and unworthy.

Before the service, a woman I'll call Lula approached me. She told me she'd battled drugs since she was sixteen. Drugs helped her deal with the reality she called her life. The thing we cling to may not be in the same form as Lula's drugs, but we've all likely grabbed hold of something and let it direct our path. How do we ask for the desire to be taken away when we've built our identity on it, when the success we think we deserve revolves around the lies we've believed? This tormented Lula. She told me she worried that if she got out of prison, she'd fall right back into drugs. But deep down, she really wanted to stop.

During the service, the Holy Spirit filled Lula. From where I sat, I watched her stand. She held up her arms and prayed aloud, "God, take my desire for the drugs away, because I can't do it alone." So many times, we find ourselves trying to do things in our own power, only to realize we just need to raise our arms.

Fifteen years ago, I walked into a prison for the first time, and I've been serving in prison ministry ever since. The woman I met at the rural health center? She's become my best friend and a part of my family. God has showered her with exceptional favor in the prison system and opened opportunities that most never receive.

We host events that bring families together, like Days with Dad and Moments with Mom, where parents and children can spend quality time together for a few precious hours. We cook meals. We create blessing bags for Christmas and distribute them. We host movie nights and other special events that remind these men and women they're seen, known, and loved.

What started as hesitation and trepidation has turned into surrender, willingness, and an obedience to show up and be where God wants me to be.

To have the opportunity to stand and watch how our Father works in the lives of those we call offenders, but those he calls sons and daughters, amazes me. They cling to each promise and believe He will deliver simply because He says He will.

Do we ever find ourselves there, wondering if He will deliver us from the everyday pitfalls we find ourselves in? I only pray that my faith is as strong as the ones I serve on the inside of those prison walls and that others will see Him in me.

I resisted the call to serve where He asked me to go. I said no, again and again. But God wouldn't let me stay comfortable. And I'm so grateful He didn't.

The Passion Translation of Psalm 139:23–24 brought everything into perspective for me: "God, I invite your searching gaze into my heart. Examine me through and through; find out everything that may be hidden within me. Put me to the test and sift through all my anxious cares. See if there is any path of pain I'm walking on, and lead me back to your glorious everlasting way, the path that brings me back to you."

Is He calling you into a mission field of unknown steps? Maybe leadership in your church, maybe being the light in your family, or maybe a ministry in the prison system serving the broken and less fortunate. Whatever ministry God is calling you to, don't be scared to take that first step. God will meet you where you are.

If you find yourself interested in prison ministry, I urge you to reach out to your local law enforcement agency. They will have resources to guide you, and God will be with you.

> Matthew 25:36 (NIV)
> I needed clothes and you clothed me, I was sick and
> you looked after me, I was in prison and you came to visit me.

SANDRA JONES is a Christian speaker and the founder of Homeless Heart Ministry. She helps women discover healing, identity, and freedom in Christ after brokenness. For more than a decade, she has shared her story at women's conferences, retreats, and inside prison walls, bringing the hope of redemption to audiences of all sizes. Sandra knows firsthand that no life is beyond God's grace, and she invites women to experience His transforming love for themselves. She's been married to her husband, Jackie, for thirty-six years, and she treasures her family, her Texas home, and a strong cup of coffee.

Connect with Sandra on her website at sandrajonesspeaks.com.

CHAPTER 4

The Surrender that Changed Everything

WHAT PLEASES GOD MOST is letting Him love us and shape us into more than we ever imagined we could become. This truth fills me with excitement because it means we get to witness God at work firsthand in our own lives.

Ephesians 2:10 (NIV) reminds us, "For we are God's handiwork created in Christ Jesus to do good works, which God prepared in advance for us to do." This verse anchors my confidence, not in my own abilities, but in who God says I am and in His unwavering faithfulness.

Life's challenges arrive with crushing weight, yet I've learned to recognize that God guides and prepares our path for His success. This recognition makes following Him far easier than attempting to handle everything alone. During trials, we begin to see that He remains constantly present, always teaching us through the challenges life presents. He speaks to us through music, through worship, and through that faithful woman whose timely words move us past our disappointments. God created us for worship and praise, and through our sorrows, we discover the strength we never knew we possessed.

Once we recognize His hand at work around us, wisdom grows, and our trust in Him deepens beyond anything we've previously experienced.

Several years ago, the lesson I needed to learn didn't originate from my own choices, but from betrayal and hurt caused by people I trusted within God's community. The pain cut so deep because I attempted to fix what only God could heal. My selfish nature refused to forgive. I walked in hurt rather than walking in obedience to God's leadership, making myself no more blameless than I pretended to be.

The realization struck me like lightning—this pain could disappear if I submitted it to the Lord, forgave those involved, and allowed God to mend my heart and redirect my focus where it needed to go. I had forgotten that He remains in control, always.

What happened was exactly what I needed: a redirection toward Jesus rather than toward myself.

The betrayal was followed by profound losses, first my sister to cancer, then my parents over the next several years. Each loss magnified every hurtful thing in life, making everything seem impossibly hard. I wondered where God was, but the truth was, I wasn't focused on Him. Scales covered my eyes for too long, and He seemed distant.

After a season of searching, I discovered He wasn't hiding. I wasn't listening or leaning on Jesus to walk through life's trials step by step. I attempted to walk alone, unable to let go because my journey wasn't pleasing to the One Who made me. I had forgotten that all these experiences might be opportunities to transform me into more than I was.

In 2021, I found myself struggling with multiple griefs simultaneously, which consisted of church hurt, losing my sister, and losing my parents.

Life as I knew it had changed, and I struggled to handle these overwhelming changes.

After weeks of crying in uncertainty, desperately believing there had to be a better way to deal with these life issues, I began to realize my life wasn't aligned with what God desired for me. I started praying earnestly, seeking Scripture, and consulting with godly women.

The breakthrough came when I learned that forgiveness for the church hurt needed to happen before I could hear God's voice clearly. I finally surrendered everything entirely to Him, forgiving completely and letting go. After all, if God could work the miracles we read about in Scripture, I knew He could work something transformative in me.

At that moment of surrender, I knew God heard my cry and changed my heart. The truth is, I had known all along that He heard me. I simply wanted a quick fix so I could move on without realizing I hadn't done my part in submission and obedience.

Only then did He give me a small vision of what was to come. He could have answered me much earlier, but it wasn't until that desperate, broken moment in my life when I finally surrendered that He could finally answer.

Looking back on this turning point, I realized I had never truly grasped what it meant to make Jesus the Lord of my life. To believe that Jesus Christ serves not only as our Savior and Teacher, but also as the Authority and Ruler of all creation. Knowing I am part of that creation, needing to be completely under His authority, changed everything.

Consider the women in Scripture who demonstrated their love for God and how pleased He was with their faithful obedience.

Mary, Jesus' mother, accepted the calling to bear God's only Son without knowing all the details. She set aside her preconceived thoughts and plans, receiving God's calling with grace. She answered, and God favored her because she accepted what He was leading her to do.

The unnamed woman in Luke 7 poured expensive perfume on Jesus' feet and wiped them with her hair. When others showed disapproval, Jesus said, "Leave her alone. She was tending to my needs." Her act of love flowed from obedience and submission because she knew who He was. Jesus accepted her service and forgave all her sins.

Esther risked her life to save her people from death. Without knowing all the details, she followed God's direction through her uncle Mordecai. Her obedience saved the Jewish people, and God answered and favored her.

Hannah prayed for a son despite being barren and dedicated him to God's service before he was even conceived. She prayed and waited for God's answer, and He favored her request.

Each woman's success in God's eyes stemmed from her obedience and commitment to serve Him faithfully.

The calling remains real, and I'm thankful Jesus used my life's storms to bring me to where I am today. I haven't arrived at perfection, but this journey has become the most incredible experience with my heavenly Father.

The dandelion serves as an excellent example of faithful perseverance. This resilient plant thrives in the toughest spots, growing even in sidewalk cracks with minimal soil. Despite harsh conditions, it continues to flourish.

It produces a bright yellow flower that transforms into a fuzzy seed head, easily whisked away by the wind to take root elsewhere and start new plants. In our circumstances, we continue with the work God guides us through to further His kingdom, going where He directs, planting His Word, and helping others grow stronger in their faith.

The dandelion's deep roots remind us of our faith in Christ and our trust in God's plan for our lives. In times of difficulty, our roots in God's love keep us strong and prevent us from being uprooted.

Like dandelion seeds, we're called to share, spread, and grow in Christ, encouraging others and bringing them into God's family. We must release the habits we've created and, like His love and guidance, allow new, healthier habits to take root.

Psalm 33:11 (NIV) declares, "But the plans of the Lord stand firm forever, the purposes of his heart through all generations." God's sovereignty and plans remain unchanging and will be accomplished.

We are created for such a place and time as this to be faithful followers, deeply rooted and perfectly placed by His design. It's the deep roots of faith that anchor us during storms, reminding us to trust in God's perfect timing and faithful provision.

The success of my story lies in my obedience to His calling. What makes anything successful in God's eyes is our willingness to be obedient, our commitment to serve, and our faithfulness to His calling, especially when the path leads through difficult terrain.

As you read this story, if you relate in any way, recognize that through God's love, He changes you. He will help you break free from old habits and transform you into what He created you to be. You are never alone in your trials, and God's glory will be revealed through your story and life lessons that can change everything for you and for someone else.

Let Jesus guide all your circumstances and lead you to serve, using you as His tool to plant seeds. The calling He has for me may differ from yours, but His love remains constant. Our purpose is to grow God's kingdom through faithful obedience to His voice.

His faithfulness never wavers, even when our circumstances seem impossible. Success in His eyes isn't measured by worldly standards, but by our willingness to trust His plan, walk in obedience, and allow Him to use our deepest trials to cultivate the strongest faith.

Isaiah 1:19 (NIV)
If you are willing and obedient, you will eat
the good things of the land.

JACKIE HAYDEN is an author, speaker, and mentor who finds joy in encouraging women through life's highs and lows. She leads a ladies' Bible study at her church and cohosts the new podcast, *Living Truth Together: Rooted & Real*. Jackie also serves as event coordinator for Rockin Retreat in East Texas and is pursuing a certificate in women's leadership from Samford University. With fifty-one years of marriage and forty-eight years of ministry alongside her husband, Ellis, she shares powerful stories of healing from church hurt and rejection. Her passion is helping women see God's hand in every season. Jackie has three grown children, five grandchildren, and her beloved Yorkie, Willow.

Connect with Jackie on her website at Jackiehaydenspeaks.com.

Chapter 5

The Power of Unseen Prayers

If you had asked me years ago what success looked like, I would have said, "A strong marriage, close friendships, peace in my home, and obtaining degrees and titles for myself." To me, that was the picture of a life well lived. But instead, I had conflict in my marriage, broken trust in friendships, and prayers that felt like they went unanswered.

For a long time, I measured success by what I could see—outcomes, changes, visible results. I spent my whole life chasing after these man-made titles, thinking that I would find happiness and success. And when I didn't see those things, I felt like I was failing. I felt like my prayers weren't working, like maybe God had forgotten about me or didn't care about me. What I didn't understand then was that God doesn't measure by appearances. He looks at faithfulness. He looks at the heart that keeps coming back to Him in prayer, even when nothing seems to change. And trust me, it seemed like things only seemed to worsen the more I prayed for them to get better.

This is the story of how seven years of unseen prayer—prayers for my husband, for friends, and my own heart—became the pathway to restoration. God was answering my prayers all along, but in His timing, not mine. And in the process, He transformed more than just relationships. He transformed me.

Our marriage wasn't easy in that season. The tension between us seemed to hang in the air like a storm cloud we couldn't escape. Some days, it felt like we were just two people sharing a roof like roommates. And instead of bringing peace, my husband's closest friendships often made things harder. His friends had a strong influence on his life, and rather than drawing us together, those relationships often drove a deeper wedge between us.

I carried a lot of hurt and anger. I wanted so badly for things to change, but it often felt like the harder I tried to fix it, the worse it became. Conversations turned into arguments, distance turned into silence, and I felt more alone than ever in my home.

There were nights when I cried myself to sleep, whispering prayers into the darkness, wondering if God was even listening. "Why aren't You doing anything? Why are You letting this continue?" From my perspective, it felt like the situation was only getting worse. We threw around the word *divorce* more than I care to admit. The one thing I had always feared going into a marriage was having kids and then getting divorced. I didn't want to put my children through what I went through as a child of parents who didn't stay married.

To others on the outside, it probably looked hopeless—a struggling marriage, with many questioning why I stayed. Strained friendships with my husband's friends, because it seemed like they were all out to get me. A wife who seemed powerless to change anything, always in a bad mood or complaining about something wrong with her marriage and husband. And in truth, that's exactly how I felt—powerless. But I didn't realize in those moments of desperation that God was not ignoring me. He was working in ways I couldn't see, laying foundations I didn't understand yet.

At the time, all I saw was the storm. But God was already preparing a testimony of restoration. And in order for that story to unfold, He was first asking me to surrender, not to my husband (I would not have done that in that particular season, and God knows I'm a stubborn lady), not to circumstances, but to Him.

Some days, prayer felt like the only thread holding me together. It wasn't polished or eloquent. Many times it was me whispering in desperation, "Lord, you better change this man. Change my heart to love him where he's at and not where I need or want him to be. Please just do something. I can't continue like this." I honestly wanted to leave and never look back.

Prayer, for me, became less about trying to control the outcome and more about choosing to obey. My father would continue to tell me to pray and mention specific areas about my husband that bothered me. That was easy to do because everything about him bothered me in those days. I wish I was exaggerating.

I wasn't a "perfect" wife either, but I was so consumed with my husband's flaws that I couldn't see my own. There were plenty of days I wanted to stop praying. After all, who keeps praying for the same thing year after year when nothing seems to change? But every time I felt ready to give up, I sensed the Spirit nudging me to keep going. So, I prayed while doing dishes. Prayed while folding the laundry. Prayed in everything I was doing. Prayed without ceasing (1 Thessalonians 5:17). It's not easy to do, especially when everything and everybody were against our marriage from day one. I felt like I was fighting a losing battle.

I didn't know why I continued in the marriage. I could've left at any time and been okay. I had my degrees to fall back on, after all. That was my escape plan going into marriage. I would always be able to take care of myself and didn't need a man. I never wanted to struggle financially, and I made sure to have a backup plan in my back pocket.

No one else saw those moments. No one else heard the prayers I prayed while washing dishes or the quiet tears I shed when I was alone. To the outside world, there was no sign of progress. There was nothing to point to and say, "It's working." But God was teaching me something deeper. He was teaching me that prayer is not wasted. That unseen faithfulness matters. That obedience, even when it feels hopeless, carries eternal weight.

So I kept praying. I prayed for my husband's heart. I prayed for his friends' hearts. And eventually, I began praying for my own heart too—that God would strip away bitterness and anger, strengthen my trust, and help me love when it felt impossible.

Those prayers weren't glamorous. Most of the time, they were covered in snot and tears running down my face. They weren't quick. I seriously questioned if God heard me. He took forever! At least it seemed like forever in my world. But prayer was the one lifeline that kept me connected to the One Who was already at work behind the scenes.

Looking back now, I can see that God was working all along, even when I couldn't physically see it. At the time, it felt like my prayers were bouncing off the ceiling. But slowly, almost imperceptibly, small shifts began to take place. My husband mentioned seeing that I was allowing Christ to work in my life. He saw the changes in me. And I saw changes in him. A softer tone in his voice. God brought good, godly friendships for my husband. Tiny glimpses that I didn't recognize as answers in the moment but that were part of God's greater plan.

One of the hardest lessons I had to learn was patience, which is funny, because I prayed for patience for seven years while riding my bike to work when we lived and worked in Germany. God's got a funny sense of humor. I wanted an overnight miracle. I wanted to wake up one morning and find everything restored, fixed, and whole. But God wasn't interested in quick fixes. He was after transformation, and true transformation takes time.

That meant God wasn't only working on the hearts of the ones I was praying for, but He was also working on mine. My prayers began to change. At first, I had been focused only on what I thought needed to happen to everyone else. But eventually, I found myself praying, "Lord, change me too." He began to peel away layers of bitterness and resentment, and He gently taught me how to release control.

The turning point wasn't a single dramatic event. It was a series of slow, steady changes that added up to something undeniable. God was softening hearts. He was drawing my husband closer to Him. He was stirring something in his best friend that only the Spirit could accomplish. And He was molding me into someone who could not only pray for them but also love them with a renewed heart.

It took seven years for God to get my husband's best friend's heart. His testimony inspired my husband to also give his heart to the Lord. Remember, I told you that God has a sense of humor? Seven long years of consistent prayers and obedience.

It didn't happen quickly. It didn't happen in the way I expected. But it happened in God's timing, and that made all the difference.

Over time, the heaviness that once filled our home began to lift. The constant tension eased, and the arguments that once seemed never-ending grew fewer. My marriage began to find a new footing, not built on resentment or mistrust, but on grace and the slow rebuilding of love. Some of the friendships that had once been a source of division also began to change. What had caused so much heartache in the past slowly became a place where God's redemption could be seen. My husband and his best friend were no longer standing in opposition to what God wanted to do; they were beginning to walk in it.

What struck me most was how God didn't just answer my prayers for them. He answered prayers I didn't even know how to pray for myself. He gave me patience when I was exhausted. He softened my heart when I was tempted to stay bitter. He taught me forgiveness, not as a one-time choice, but as a daily practice.

The restoration wasn't dramatic or flashy. There was no single moment where everything instantly became perfect. Instead, it was a slow and steady healing, the kind only God can orchestrate. And in many ways, that made it even more beautiful. Because it showed me His timing is not only perfect; it's purposeful.

What I've learned through this journey is that God's work often looks different from what we expect. I thought I needed quick answers, visible change, and proof that my prayers were working. But God was after something deeper and a lasting transformation, not temporary relief.

For seven years, my prayers felt unseen. But heaven saw them. And in God's time, those quiet, persistent prayers became the seeds of restoration. He changed my husband. He changed some of his friends' hearts. And perhaps, most importantly, He changed me.

I now see that faithfulness in a hidden place is never wasted. Prayer is never wasted. Even when it feels like nothing is happening, God is moving in ways we cannot yet see.

So if you find yourself in a season of waiting, keep praying. Keep trusting. Keep leaning into God's timing. Because what may feel silent and unseen here on earth is fully seen and treasured in heaven. And when the time is right, God's answer will be far more beautiful than anything you could have imagined.

> Romans 12:12 (NIV)
>
> Be joyful in hope, patient in affliction, faithful in prayer.

ASHLY GEMMILL is a wife, mom, and Army spouse who understands the ups and downs of faith, family, and finding your place when life feels uncertain. With a heart for women who feel unseen, rejected, or weighed down, she loves creating safe and honest spaces where healing can begin.

Ashly enjoys teaching Bible studies, writing, and sharing her story in ways that remind women they are not alone. Her hope is to walk alongside others as they rediscover their worth in Christ and experience His unchanging love. Whether it's through speaking, teaching, or simply sharing coffee with a friend, Ashly's passion is pointing women back to the One Who never left them.

Connect with Ashly at standupstandoutwithashly@gmail.com.

CHAPTER 6

Click

IN MY SOPHOMORE YEAR of high school, I decided to run track. My best athletic friend, Diane, ran for the team. Why couldn't I? It was just running. I was an expert at wearing red lipstick, blue eyeshadow, and feathering my hair so perfectly you could hear a resounding hallelujah from the heavenlies. I thought, "How hard could it be?" Have you ever been wrong in your thinking?

I often think about those days and laugh at the warm-ups and practices that completely wore me out long before the actual race, the five-mile runs in the afternoons just to prepare me to run one leg of the relay race, and I will not even mention the weight room. What did lifting arm weights have to do with running? You are getting the picture.

I still laugh when I remember those stormy days running timed laps in the school gym. Our coach had one of those lap counters with the clicking noise. You may have just heard that sound in your own mind—the simple click that marks each completed lap. But to me, it sounded like an air-raid siren when I finished one lap and got one click while my teammates had already rounded the corner of the gym for their fifth.

I remember a particular day when I was struggling. My coach yelled out, "Keep going, Cherie! It's not the number of clicks you get, it's that you finish your lap and receive a click. Finish!"

Those words still resonate with me. Having been in ministry for the past twenty-three years, I often equated high audience attendance and paychecks with a measure of affirmation from God that I was on the right track. This time, not physical running but running the spiritual race outlined in Hebrews. Today, you may be struggling too. Are you finding it hard to manage the world's defined successes? The unachievable beliefs about motherhood, careers, ministry, your children's behavior, and the Mother Superior of all titles, the title of being a Proverbs 31 woman. I am sure I could have been a Proverbs 32 woman if that chapter existed.

This past July, I was speaking at an event in Grand Rapids, Michigan. After the conference, my husband and our beloved friends—yes, Diane, the runner and her husband—met up with me to travel together to Mackinac Island. Our trip was beautiful. During our last two days, we drove back down toward Grand Rapids to fly back home. But air travel had a hitch we did not see coming because our airline app on our phone said our flight was on time.

A hamburger, French fries, M&M's, and trail mix later, there was no plane in sight. As we stood in the crowded gate, awaiting the over-three-hour-delayed flight of our first leg home to Charlotte, NC, a gentleman hurriedly walking toward the gate caught my eye. The young man began to jog toward the gates. Can I add here that an attractive young man rushed directly toward me? He then called out loudly, "Is anyone traveling to Charlotte?"

I immediately responded with a Southern-charmed twang, "Why, yes, I am."

Knowing me very well, my husband rolled his eyes and said, "Really?"

I chuckled, and the young man walked over to me and said, "There is an elderly couple needing to fly into Charlotte, and they are confused. Can you see to it they get on their plane? My flight is to Chicago, and it is boarding right now."

I turned and looked at the couple, and they were a little older than old. They were more like elderly. The precious woman was pushing a gentleman in a wheelchair, and I responded, "Certainly, I will."

I walked over to the couple and assured them they were at the right gate, but that was not enough to appease them. Following twenty questions and a DNA swab, they decided to accept me. I led them to sit down at the gate and assured them that we should be boarding our plane, which had not arrived, shortly.

That shortly became another hour. I walked over to them multiple times to check on them and learned sweet stories about this couple. They were newlyweds. You heard it. They married a year prior after both had previously lost their spouses years earlier. Having been prom dates in the past, they later reconnected. After the plane landed and we were getting ready to board, I quickly checked on them before they were escorted onto the aircraft. I asked, "Are you ready?"

The precious lady then responded, "No, my husband has lost his phone."

Both individuals appeared disorganized, and I assisted them in searching through their possessions. No phone—just credit cards, gum, and mints. I asked them what the phone looked like. She then pulled out her flip phone, which was identical to his, and said, "It looks just like this one."

I thought they had purchased them at the turn of the century, but kept my thoughts to myself. I then assured them the phone would not be expensive to replace, and they should contact their carrier to put his phone line on hold. I thought for a second and then asked myself, "What do I do on these occasions?" I said, "Have you tried calling his phone?"

She smiled and replied, "What a great idea!"

She dialed his phone, and a ring tone bellowed from his bag tucked under his wheelchair. I reached under his wheelchair, retrieved the phone, and we all chuckled. They thanked me, and I walked back over to my husband and our friends.

The airline began boarding military and those in need of assistance first, but as she pushed him to the line, she looked over at me, stroked her hand over her forehead, and mouthed. "Whew!" I smiled, but her next motion took my breath away. She cupped her hands as if she were praying, bowed toward me, and pursed her lips again to say, "Thank you!"

The next sound I heard was a divine *click.* I finished my lap that day. Oh, not in record time, but in the time God marked out for me.

Our spiritual race is not about paychecks and large audiences. The kingdom of Heaven is built one person at a time. A grandiose audience and the paycheck of paychecks are not God's measure of ministering to others. Being successful in God's eyes is the day-to-day perseverance of running our race that is marked out for us by God. If we listen daily, we will hear the wonder of the click.

> Hebrews 12:1–2 (NIV)
> Therefore, since we are surrounded by such a great cloud of witnesses, let us throw off everything that hinders and the sin that so easily entangles. And let us run with perseverance the race marked out for us.

CHERIE NETTLES is a comedienne, motivational speaker, and Bible teacher who helps women discover the healing power of joy, even in life's hardest seasons. A certified Laughter Leader and twenty-three-year ovarian cancer survivor, Cherie has overcome childhood abuse, chronic illness, and heartbreak with faith and humor. Her story reminds women that joy is not an option—it is a weapon. Known for her Southern sass and bold red lipstick, she brings hope and hilarity to stages across the United States.

Connect with Cherie on her website at cherienettles.com.

Chapter 7

Never Say Never

Being called to the principal's office can be daunting, even if you're in your mid-forties and a teacher. I had come to my classroom to pick up textbooks in preparation for my role as kindergarten team leader when school reopened in August. Mr. Rains, the elementary principal, stuck his head in my room and asked if I would come to his office for a few minutes. Sitting on the opposite side of his desk, I sensed a serious conversation coming. Shifting in the leather chair, trying to find a comfortable position, I wondered if he heard my heart thumping. Finally, he cleared his throat, "Ms. Chitsey, you are the new art teacher for junior high this coming year."

It felt as if someone had punched the air out of my lungs. I was stunned by his words, and tears streamed down my face. I didn't know what to say as my thoughts ran rampant. "Me, teach junior high." I said, "I would never teach students of this age. It's out of my comfort zone. The biggest drawback is that I hate confrontation of any sort. Working with adolescents as they begin puberty and trying to act grown-up would be an open door to only God knows what kinds of controversies."

After a few moments, my thoughts slowed down, and I regained my composure. I remember looking up and smiling the best I could, after all, it was a done deal. Mr. Rains' kind eyes met mine; his body language showed he dreaded telling me the news. He offered a tissue. I took one and dried my cheeks. Focusing on the rest of our conversation became a challenge because his words seemed garbled and unclear. Not literally, but because of the shock I had just endured.

Back in my classroom, I sat at my desk and replayed the last twenty minutes in my mind over and over. I finally gathered my things and went home. The world I had known over the previous twenty-four years of teaching in elementary had instantly disappeared forever.

The administration assigned me to teach art to seventh- and eighth-grade students, as well as a new curriculum called Teen Leadership, for all eighth-grade students. Half of the students received instruction in the fall and the other half in the spring.

That day, I learned an important life lesson: "You never say never ... "

Because God, in His humorous but loving way, may reply, "I'll just see about that." For instance, my husband picked me up for our first date wearing blue-striped bell-bottoms, a blue-striped shirt, white patent-leather shoes, and a white leather belt. I shook my head and thought, "This will never work." We've been married fifty-three years.

As a Texas educator, I am bound by a contract that states I could be placed in any position the school district needs to be filled. I hold both a bachelor's and a master's degree in elementary education, with a minor in art, which meets the qualifications for my new job description.

Returning home, I prayed, asking the Lord why. Why? Why? With tear ducts depleted from crying, I felt the presence of the Holy Spirit whisper,

"Go look at your New Year's resolutions." But where had I written my resolutions? I immediately found the sketchbook. In black ink on the front cover of the book was the list. I scanned it. Number seventeen jumped off the page. "Use my artistic ability." Nodding, I smiled. I had requested, and the Lord answered.

It took a few moments to put the puzzle pieces together and understand the Lord's confirmation of my new teaching position. I couldn't deny it, and in fact, I felt a bit giddy because being an art teacher aligned with a subject I loved: creativity. When I was a child, Daddy showed me how to draw horses and dogs, which always looked like they were trying to sit down. My mother taught me to sketch paper dolls and their outfits, a memory that still brings a smile to my face. In the sixth grade, I began sewing my own clothes, and later, I dreamed of becoming a renowned fashion designer. Instead of that dream, God fulfilled another as I married my high school sweetheart after graduation and attended college to receive my teaching degree, where I was finally able to take formal art lessons and even minor in the field. God always had a plan to use my creativity in ways I never dreamed possible.

As I closed down my kindergarten classroom, I discarded most of my elementary teaching guides, books, and supplies. I trusted the Lord's plan, which He confirmed with the proof in my handwriting.

Our entire school district is situated on a single campus, and moving to the junior high building was like taking a giant leap for *teacher-kind*. I felt like an astronaut going to a new planet, pulling my children's old Radio Flyer wagon across the cement walkway, loaded with all the items I chose to keep from my teaching days in elementary school.

The feeling of isolation was real that summer. School was out, my teaching friends were enjoying their break, and none of them knew about my new assignment. I felt very much alone, but I found comfort in my current classroom, which was my old home economics room. On the brighter side, my new principal was very generous and let me plan and order any art medium I needed. I was also free to design my own curriculum.

My overall goal while serving in this new position was to introduce these junior high students to various types of art projects that would last a lifetime. Teaching art was fun, but at times frustrating when students didn't realize how fortunate they were even to have art in school. I would have taken every opportunity to explore and express my creativity if it had been offered when I attended school. My students' favorite project was sewing a small pillow. They traced their hand and embroidered it onto the fabric and then stuffed the pillow with batting. They loved their pillows. Some students kept them in their lockers and used them in their other classes during free time. Strangely enough, I do believe the boys always did the best handwork.

I also taught a class called Teen Leadership to all the eighth graders. I truly believe this was the real target area the Lord wanted me to work with. The curriculum resembled a character education class, which sometimes brought opportunities for confrontation with a few of the more verbal and rebellious teens. To my disappointment, I clashed with a few of my former students who dearly loved me in the lower grades.

I spent many hours scouring the internet to find art lessons and activities for the Teen Leadership class. Through my research, I discovered a tool that helped us all: journaling. We journaled to release all the junk we stuff down inside ourselves and try to keep secret. I assigned an activity to write a letter to someone they admired. A few students chose a family member who had died. Talk about a tear-jerker. In conjunction with journaling, I encouraged students to talk to people they trusted, a pet, or even a stuffed animal. It didn't matter as long as they verbalized their emotions aloud to release the pain associated with a bad experience. In the end, journaling became more than just an assignment. It was a lifeline that provided my students (and me) a safe place to process, release, and navigate life's ups and downs.

Teaching Teen Leadership gave me countless positive experiences, though a handful of moments tested my patience and resolve. An unforgettable experience occurred while modeling the proper way to greet people. Every day, Teen Leadership teachers were expected to stand at the door to welcome students, maintain eye contact, and offer a firm handshake. Most students were fine with this, but a few disliked it and often put up a fuss.

On a particular Friday at the beginning of the last period, a student walked up to me, licked her hand, and then offered it for a handshake. I stood there, shocked and speechless; however, I managed to say, "No, thank you." To the best of my ability, I blocked this incident for the rest of the period and didn't report it to the principal until Monday morning. During the weekend, that confrontational scene replayed constantly in my mind. I decided not to let the student get away with disrespecting a teacher's position, no matter who they happened to be. Whether or not her reprimand from the principal made an impression, only God knows. Obviously, it has had a lasting impression on me. Even so, the joy of watching my students grow and flourish far surpassed the sting of that one unforgettable exchange.

Being able to face my fear of teaching junior high-aged students definitely pushed me out of my comfort zone. It enabled me to go where I had never gone before. It also gave me the courage to say yes when God invited me to new experiences, like traveling on mission trips to Jamaica with my Teen Leadership students. My first trip included twenty-one students, and it set the stage for five more journeys to follow. I always encouraged them to step out of their comfort zone, so I needed to do the same.

I've already mentioned that God has a sense of humor. I have numerous testimonies of God using my creative talent in comedic ways on this small island. On the first day in Jamaica, our bus arrived at the community center, where the mission organization had been working in collaboration with other churches. I panicked after spying the homemade scaffold put together with sticks and rope, which a gust of wind could blow away at any moment. I'm sure God gave a big ole belly laugh when my eyes became the size of saucers, and I thought, "Oh Lord, do you really want me to climb on that thing to work?" Thankfully, I didn't have to actually climb the scaffold.

I was blessed beyond measure when, on another trip, I was asked to design and paint a mural inside the community center. With the help of other team members and some Jamaican boys, we created a six-foot replica of the world and then painted the Scripture John 3:16 (NASB). "For God so loved the world that He gave his only Son ..." It still amazes me to think that something as simple as our painting has become a lasting witness to the gospel—one that continues to speak to others long after our team went home.

My teaching assignment for junior high students lasted nine years, and if I had a choice, I would do it again because I grew as a person, in my faith, in my art, and in my new chapter of life, which is writing and public speaking. Becoming a junior high teacher when I was really an elementary teacher was difficult, especially when I felt as if I was alone on a new planet. To add to my isolation, I didn't have a team to work with, unlike the other teachers. Additionally, since I was a newbie, I hadn't built the kind of friendships or connections that helped me feel a part of the group. But I knew God was right there beside me. Let me reiterate that if I had to do it all over again, I would say yes because the struggles in my life helped shape me into the person the Lord intended me to be before He formed me in my mother's womb.

I have enjoyed the gifts and talents He has given me throughout my life. In His eyes, I am a success when I choose to follow His will for my life. Success is knowing Who holds our hand when we fall or when we fail. The Lord will always be available 24/7 when we call out His name. The words I want to hear when I enter the pearly gates of heaven are "Well done, my good and faithful servant" (Matthew 25:21 NLT).

Proverbs 16:3 (NLT)

Commit your actions to the Lord, and your plans will succeed.

After accepting Jesus as Lord and Savior at the age of nine, JOY MICHELE CHITSY recalls the moment standing in her Grandma Hunter's driveway, with the sun shining brightly, thinking about becoming a missionary. She has worked in several mission areas as a daughter, sister, friend, wife, mother, grandmother (GoGo), teacher, artist, writer, speaker, prayer warrior, and she's even been on out-of-country mission trips.

Michele shares personal stories of how God provides strength, wisdom, hope, forgiveness, mercy, and encouragement to pass along to the people He puts in her path. She is the author of *John 3:16 Messengers* and the coauthor, with Trish Kuhl, of *Jingle Your Jolly*, and has more on the way.

Her passion is journaling, and she teaches women the importance of leaving a legacy of love through journaling. Her favorite song is "Jesus Loves Me."

Connect with Michele at joymichelechitsey@gmail.com.

CHAPTER 8

Our Obedience and Partnership with God to Fulfill His Plans and Purpose

IN 2003, APPROXIMATELY SIXTY percent of those who experienced a hemorrhagic stroke did not survive. Among the survivors, only twenty percent went on to live an independent life, six months post-stroke. I shouldn't be here, but I am, and that's just the beginning of how God rewrote my story. My survival and ability to thrive in this new normal have been a journey of discovery of God's purpose and plans, which are far greater than any plans I ever dreamed for myself.

Prior to my stroke, I worked in a corporate setting, with a background in business and marketing. However, two of my greatest desires were to be a mom and use my skills in a more purpose-driven arena than corporate America. I decided to switch my focus to church, and I was offered the position of office manager. I thought this was an avenue to both slow my life down for motherhood and have a more purpose-driven career. I had no idea that this was the beginning of a much bigger journey than just a career change.

When I made this career change, I was unaware that I was a walking time bomb in terms of my health condition. As far as I knew, I was a healthy twenty-nine-year-old who worked out several times a week. However, three weeks into this new church career, I suffered a massive hemorrhagic stroke caused by an undiagnosed birth defect. God chose this moment when He knew I was in a safe place for the malformation of blood vessels to rupture. So, the employment change was God's plan to protect me.

It started with a horrible headache and an upset stomach. My left arm felt heavy all morning. At these first signs, I called my husband and parents, who lived nearby. Then, my left leg went numb, so a coworker called 911 for help. The last conversation I remember having was an offer to give my insurance card to the paramedics. Then the lights went out. My health deteriorated quickly, and I was unconscious within an hour of our initial 911 call.

My mom was a passenger in the ambulance on the way to the hospital, and at one point, the radio dispatcher asked, "How far out are you from the hospital?"

The driver responded, "Too far. I don't think we will make it in time." As an only child, I can't imagine the emotions my mom must have been processing from the time she received my phone call to when she was riding in the ambulance. What happened to her little girl was completely out of her control.

Thankfully, we arrived at the hospital in time. After they diagnosed the problem at the hospital and got me into an emergency brain surgery to stop the brain bleed, I was placed in a drug-induced coma for seventeen days to keep my brain pressure down. When they woke me up, I realized I had no movement on my left side. I wish I were one of those survivors who had memories of my time in a coma or vivid thoughts when I first came out. Unfortunately, I don't. Some of my first memories were confusion, fear, and wondering how I was ever going to fulfill my desire to be a mom if only half my body now worked. From the very beginning of my stroke recovery journey, I was like the Energizer Bunny with rechargeable batteries, yearning to get better and doing as much therapy as the hospital therapists would allow.

There are so many little things I recall from those days in the hospital. Going to the bathroom and taking a shower was no longer a private affair, so any sense of modesty was immediately diminished. I was such a people pleaser that I hesitated to bother a nurse and ask her to do her job to help me. Through that time, I learned the importance of finding the small things I could control and being joyful about them. One of the simple pleasures that gave me joy was going to the ice machine. Pushing the button for ice was something I had control over.

We all go through many challenges that we have no control over. But we always have a choice in our reaction to our circumstances. Choosing our attitude, perspective, and dependence on God through those trials may not change the physical challenge, but it can alter our outlook on the situation and ultimately enhance our ability to overcome it. I would have never imagined I'd be in a hospital for two months, have to undergo an eleven-hour brain surgery, or still have disabilities to deal with today, but God has helped me weather every storm and has been my constant protector, ally, and strength.

By eight years post-stroke, we decided we still really wanted a family, so we embarked on an international adoption to bring home a sibling group of three. Because of my epilepsy, disability, involvement with Compassion International Ministries, and a calling to give older children a forever family that might never have one, this avenue towards family planning made the most sense. We were blessed with three beautiful children, and I will always be grateful for the opportunity to be a mom. We endured more trauma and challenges than we were prepared for, especially after my medical journey. However, I learned a great deal from each experience, and God gave me the perspective that every challenge can be an opportunity. I can now support others with empathy, rather than sympathy, drawing on my medical and parenting experiences.

During the pandemic, I felt a nudge to start writing and sharing with others all that I had learned from my stroke recovery, adoption, and parenting experiences. My first book was published in 2022, and as I began sharing my journey with others, I learned a great deal, reentering the big, unsheltered world. I tried to support and encourage others the way I always needed to be supported. However, I realized that, as a people pleaser, not everyone gives or receives in the same way I do. I also learned that many of my friends were unable to understand and support me the way my heart longed to be supported. It wasn't their lack of care or love but their lack of relatability.

My grief and loneliness for a friend to understand and support me were unwarranted, because God was standing by my side all along, just waiting for me to be ready to acknowledge and partner with Him. Have you ever gone through a tough trial and yearned for a good friend to say the one thing that resonated with your soul, helping you know you weren't alone? There is only One Who can completely understand our exact footsteps and soothe the hurts of our souls, and that is the God Who created us. It took me a long time to reach that place of understanding and depending on Him first. I spent years shutting down because I thought no one understood. I now realize that my vulnerability lies in connecting, helping, encouraging, and supporting others. But my partnership with God has shown me that He is the friend I always longed for.

My prayer request and desire of my heart prior to my stroke was to have a more purpose-filled career. God heard that prayer. He never left me. He chose to let me live through a massive stroke, give me skills to thrive in this new normal, and gift me the miracles of survival for His plans.

Those plans include a disability to this day. Those plans also include continued medical challenges so that I continue to depend on Him and stay humble as I share with others. God has given me incredible experiences that surpass my imagination so that I can encourage others and share the hope and joy in the midst of medical trials and continued challenges. With God by our side, He can take our mess and help us turn it into a message to encourage just the right individual.

Where the world often looks at success through the lens of being a people pleaser and how to meet the next person's expectations, my medical challenges and adoption and parenting journey gave me the greatest gift I could have asked for. It was the gift of dependence on God, rather than myself, that allowed me to truly understand what true joy looks like, as opposed to the fleeting emotion of worldly happiness.

As I continue discovering God's plans for me, I am in constant amazement at how His purpose prevails. Today, I live a fuller and more joy-filled life than I did before my medical journey began. We often cannot control the challenges we face, but we do have a choice in how we react to our circumstances. To think that God views success as simply taking His hand in obedience with no expectations, partnering with Him, and trusting in His plans, no matter what the outcome, is both beautiful and peaceful.

Many people look at and quote Jeremiah 29:11, but I love Jeremiah 29:11–13 (NIV), which says, "'For I know the plans I have for you,' declares the Lord, 'plans to prosper you and not to harm you, plans to give you hope and a future. Then you will call on me and come and pray to me, and I will listen to you. You will seek me and find me when you seek me with all your heart.'" God has great plans for each of us. When we choose to seek Him and find Him with our whole heart, then our whole world changes forever. That is when God's plans and purpose become our compass for our journeys.

I am thankful to have found my Best Friend in the One Who created me. I'm never alone. You aren't either.

We're successful in His eyes when we finally reach a point of surrender of our own plans and will, and we are ready to partner with God to fulfill the purpose and plans He has for our lives.

> Proverbs 19:21 (NIV)
> Many are the plans in a person's heart,
> but it is the Lord's purpose that prevails.

LORI VOBER is a motivational speaker, published author, hemorrhagic stroke survivor, adoptive mom, and a woman who refuses to quit.

As a woman who has faced infertility, stroke recovery, epilepsy, and other unplanned medical challenges, Lori chooses to find hope, joy, and a new tomorrow when faced with the challenges of today. She is passionate about bringing hope and encouragement to stroke survivors and others who have experienced unexpected challenges.

Lori encourages others as a speaker in a variety of settings, from stroke support groups to church events and retreats. She has a wealth of experience from her journey as a stroke survivor and an adoptive mom of three older children.

You can find Lori's first award-winning book, *CHOICES: When You Are Faced with a Challenge, What Choice Will You Make?*, along with her other compilations and speaking examples on her website.

Connect with Lori on her website at lorivober.com.

WORTHY

Chapter 9

Never Enough

I CAN REMEMBER HOW my siblings and I were introduced as young girls. It always started with my oldest sister. "This is Sheila. She is so smart. Then Sandy, she is the shy, sweet one. Then Sheri, such a natural beauty. And then this is Sonia. She's the youngest, the baby of the family."

Now I don't think anything was meant by it, but still, to my young heart, that's all I heard. The youngest? I wasn't smart enough, sweet enough, or pretty enough to have those adjectives; I was simply the youngest. I think it set my feet on the path to never feeling like I was enough in anything. The enemy does that, doesn't he? He will take things said in our presence and twist them in our minds. It seemed no matter how hard I tried, I could never be smart enough, sweet enough, or pretty enough. I always fell short.

In school, no matter how hard I tried to stay focused and study to make good grades, I never walked away with all As or even As and Bs; I got a C or worse on my report card every time.

And my personality? You know, there are people who, as we say in the South, are just sugar-dripping sweet. Well, I didn't inherit those genes. I had a temper that I couldn't seem to control and a smart mouth, as my mama would say.

I also fell short in the looks department. My sisters all had hair that was more of a deep golden blond, while mine was brown—boring brown. Once, we had chalk drawings done of our profiles to give to our mom as a gift. My sisters, all three of them, had the prettiest golden hair in those drawings; mine was brown, and my profile was not nearly as soft and pretty as theirs. Theirs showed a femininity about them that mine just didn't have. I loved their drawings, but I thought mine was just boring and, quite frankly, ugly.

I didn't grow up in church. I can remember being the pet project for the VBS ladies. Every year, they knocked on our door to ask if I could come to VBS. I found that I really loved it there, even though I had no clue what they were talking about most of the time.

I could never make the cut in school either; it seemed I was not good at sports or activities. I was always the last one picked, or worse, not picked at all, because the numbers for the team ran out before I was picked. It also helped to set me up for the feeling I have had for the rest of my life. I was never enough.

I gave my heart to Jesus when I was fifteen. I knew He had something I wanted, but I wasn't quite sure how to get there. Back in the seventies, at least in my little church, discipleship was not high on the list. Once you were saved, it was just assumed that you knew what to do next. I didn't understand the Bible stories. I still remember my thoughts the first time I heard the story about some guy getting swallowed by a fish and spit out three days later. But I was too afraid to ask questions, because I was afraid people would know that I was not enough. I drifted in and out of my faith over the next few years. However, I always felt drawn back to Jesus, Scripture, and His church.

Somehow, I lucked up and married a very handsome fella that I truly believe God handpicked for me, even though I know I did not consult Him about it. About ten months after our wedding date, we had our first child. I was a mama, and it scared me to death. I barely had time to learn to be a wife before I was a mama. I never felt I knew what to do when my kids were sick or needed a sweet little lesson. I seemed to always miss those "teachable moments" that other mamas were so good at.

To add to my "not enough" syndrome, I am not the best housekeeper. I'm not a good cook, and my house is cluttered. Not nasty, but I might have to move things off the sofa if you came for a visit. I seemed to always fall short in every department.

But ... almost thirty years ago now, in 1998, I felt some of the trajectory of these feelings begin to shift. I was a young mama with two kids, and I recall sitting in church when the idea of a daily quiet time, a walk with Jesus, began to penetrate my thoughts. Sunday after Sunday, our Pastor talked about how we needed to build a relationship with Jesus.

One day, he said, "It is just as much your responsibility to know that what I am speaking from the pulpit is truth as it is mine to speak it."

That hit me hard! I didn't know Scripture, not very well, and the idea of this relationship thing was foreign to me. I knew I was saved, but what was he talking about? I have a cousin who, at the time, was singing in a traveling gospel quartet, and his group stayed in our home one night when they passed through. As we talked on the sofa, he said, "Isn't walking with Jesus the sweetest thing?"

I said, "Uh-huh." And in my mind, I thought, "What is he talking about?" I heard this over and over in sermons, conversations, and even on the Christian radio station I listened to. That's what we used to do before we had all the music and podcasts on our phones.

About the same time, my best friend was going through an unwanted divorce. I offered to keep her children for her. We were stay-at-home moms together, but she was going back to work so she could support her children. I knew I was going to need some strength and reinforcement, and my interest had been piqued! So, I enrolled in a couple of Bible studies, bought a book about prayer and a notebook, and decided to start spending an hour a day in prayer with Jesus.

Goodness gracious, the first day I read a passage in my Bible, a short chapter in my book, and opened my little notebook for prayer. I was about twenty minutes in with my reading behind me, which meant I had forty minutes left to pray if I was going to spend a whole hour on this. My prayer took about five minutes, maybe. *What do I do? What do I tell Him that He doesn't already know?* I stared at the blank page. I had no idea what to write or where to go with this. I fell short again.

But for the first time in my life, I didn't let it derail me. I wrote out a verse:

"Ask, and it will be given to you; seek, and you will find; knock, and it will be opened to you. For everyone who asks receives, and the one who seeks finds, and to the one who knocks it will be opened" Matthew 7:7–8 (NASB).

I wrote a list of prayer requests, and then I just very simply wrote a letter to God. I asked Him to help me with my commitment. I prayed for my husband and my kids. I prayed for my friend and her children. I prayed for a friend, whom I knew was walking in a lifestyle against what he knew to be right, to have conviction in his heart. I prayed for prayer requests I heard at church, and I prayed again for myself ... that I could stick with this.

The next day, I showed up again. I read my Bible. I wrote out a verse, listed my prayer list, and wrote my letter to God. It didn't take me an hour, even though that was my goal. But I was determined not to fall short in this. I rolled out of bed around 5:00 every morning, because keeping the children started at about 6:30 a.m., which was hard for this girl who was not a morning person. One day, I got to the door of my bedroom, and I almost turned around to go back to bed. But I stomped my foot and said, "Satan, you are not going to get me to give up on this!"

Over time, I prayed for friends to have babies. I prayed for my children's friendships. I prayed for godly wives for them, even though they were only eight and three years old at the time. Every morning, I read, wrote out a Bible verse or a praise chorus, and wrote my letter to God. It was very simple.

I prayed that one day I would know and understand Scripture, and I would fall in love with His Word. But I didn't feel very smart, so I just didn't know that I would ever really measure up. And then I ran across a verse. It was like an arrow to my soul. "The Law of the Lord is perfect, restoring the soul; The testimony of the Lord is sure, making wise the simple" Psalm 19:7 (NASB).

"Lord, is that possible for even me?" I began to pray the verse over my quiet time. I wanted to know Scripture, to understand it so that I could help others know and understand it. I wanted to fall in love with it, and I wanted to encourage others to fall in love with it too. I wondered, "Could diving into Scripture really help make this girl with a simple mind, who couldn't measure up, wise?" Some of my early prayers were for the Lord to give me a love for His word so that I could teach and recall Scripture like I saw other godly women do.

Then one day, a year or two into this journey, I was in the elevator at church heading to worship from Sunday school, and another woman from our class was on the elevator with me, and she made a comment to me I've never forgotten. She said, "Sonia, I just wish I knew these Bible stories the way you do." I was stunned and a little proud of how far I had come. The little girl who wasn't sure she bought the story of Jonah and the whale was told by another that she had impressed her with her Bible knowledge.

Over time, my prayer time has grown, and now on some days, I may even spend a couple of hours in my quiet time with Jesus. I have found that time with Jesus has truly helped me battle those little voices in my head that were so ingrained in my thought processes. I found verses that told me I was fearfully and wonderfully made. And a verse that said He would take our ashes and turn them into beauty. I was so awestruck by what I was learning that I wanted to keep at it. I wanted to keep digging, and I wouldn't believe the lies of the enemy who told me over and over that I would never measure up and may as well give up.

I can honestly say that, over time, God has given this simple-minded girl more understanding of His Word. I still struggle with Scripture memory and the address at times. But He has given me opportunities to teach and stand before small groups of women and tell them how much I love Jesus and His Word. I began to resurrect the dreams I had of writing and started writing devotions and posting them online. And much to my surprise, people actually read them!

I still struggle sometimes with not feeling like enough. I can find myself walking into a room with strong, capable women, wondering what I am doing there, praying for the Lord to beam me up and take me back to my lake and let me just hang out there so I can become an eccentric old woman who grows tomatoes, wears funny hats, writes, and paints. But that's not *really* what I want. I still pray to let others see Him and to find a love for His Word in me. And He shows me that if I keep my eyes completely focused on Him, then the success of anything I do, whether I write, speak, or paint, is complete in His eyes. To me, success is my obedience to Him, to study, to pray, to give Him all of me, and to let Him lead, guide, and direct me. It truly does not matter what the world thinks of me.

I wish I could tell you the "who does she think she is" voices were always silent. They aren't, but they are quieter than they once were, and I know now that all I have to do is go to Jesus and listen to what He says about me. That is how to silence them. I know that when I keep my eyes on Him, He sees me as successful, and that makes all things possible.

> Philippians 4:13 (NASB)
> I can do all things through Him who strengthens me.

SONIA STICKER has been a writer at heart for as long as she can remember. After years of journaling and quietly dreaming of writing books, a simple sentence from a podcast, "If you want to be a writer, you must write," stirred her into action. When the world shut down, Sonia posted daily devotionals on Facebook, and to her surprise, others read and resonated with them.

Driven by a personal hunger for deeper biblical understanding, Sonia is passionate about helping other women pursue biblical literacy for themselves. She is a Bible teacher, certified speaker, singer, and amateur artist whose greatest desire is to help others fall in love with Jesus and His Word.

Connect with Sonia on her website at soniasticker.com.

CHAPTER 10

Worth So Much More

WHO CAN YOU TALK to when your marriage takes a deep dive, *and* your husband is the pastor?

Practically born on the church pew three rows back from the altar, my family never missed a chance to be in church. I started learning Scripture as a child. Our pastor made sure I understood salvation, and my youth group was like no other. They were my best friends. Many of us still stay in touch. The churches my parents chose to attend provided godly examples of adult leaders.

One year, I took a class about sharing our testimonies. I never felt mine was good enough. We were to tell about our lives before Christ, how we came to know Christ, and what our lives were like after Christ. In the early years of elementary school, I made the decision to ask Jesus to be my Savior. The one word that described my life before Christ was *good*. But it didn't matter how good I was because I could never be good enough. I needed a Savior, just like everyone else. I learned during that class that my testimony *was* good enough, because I wasn't. I could share with others that being good doesn't save you. The years that followed were full of setting a scriptural foundation for life.

Being raised in a service-oriented Christian home and taught to study the Bible, the foundation of truth—this was success. Then I married a preacher. Double success, at least in the eyes of the Christian community, which was all I knew. My career desire was to find a position in a support role. I dreamed of having a Christian husband, a peaceful home, the proverbial white picket fence, 2.3 children, and a dog. I couldn't have asked for a better life, supporting a husband in the ministry while raising my children in a Christian home.

The first signs of trouble came on our wedding day. As my daddy lowered my veil and prepared to walk me down the aisle, I felt as if a hundred butterflies were flittering around inside. Was I doing the right thing? Of course, I was. This was a dream come true. I was about to become a pastor's wife and could not wait to serve God with my new husband. Besides, it was time to walk down the aisle. Why would I question this now? Wedding day jitters, for sure.

Breathe in. Breathe out. Release the fluttering inside. All was well in my life.

After the reception, we headed to a hotel on the beach to spend our honeymoon. My beautiful wedding bouquet rested on a pillow in the back seat. On the way, we stopped at a convenience store. When we returned to the car, my new husband, who pledged to love, honor, and cherish me, threw a bottle of Sprite into the back seat and onto the delicate flowers. I let out a shriek. "The flowers!"

As he watched me climb over the front seat to move the bottle and save the flowers, he said, "It's just a bunch of flowers. It's not a big deal."

My jaw dropped as if someone had punched me in the gut, and all the butterflies I released earlier flew back into the pit of my stomach.

They were just flowers, yes, but they represented so much more. They represented promises. They represented dreams. They represented the blooms of years to come. I didn't realize it then, but just a bunch of flowers would lead to just a bunch of lies and unfulfilled dreams. Promises, dreams, and years that would never come. As the flowers in the bouquet died, so would the vows that never really lived.

One day, he walked out the door after another argument, but he left his wallet. As I opened the wallet and stood questioning what I found, the doorknob rattled and the back door squeaked. He had returned.

"What makes you think you can go through my wallet?" Somehow, everything always became my fault. He pushed me against the edge of the kitchen counter, grabbed the carving fork from the knife block, and placed it against my throat. After a minute, he tossed the fork aside.

"You aren't worth it."

He picked up his wallet and walked out the back door.

Somewhere in the recesses of my mind, I heard a still, small voice saying, "No, you are worth so much more."

Another argument, each one becoming more physical. I couldn't do anything right. Once again, we were fighting, and I didn't even know why. It was all so pointless. I stumbled. He pushed me, and I fell. I curled into a ball to protect myself from what might come. He kicked me, spat on me, and told me I was worthless. Then he turned and walked out the door.

I lay on the living room carpet crying. I felt my heart bleeding, but it was an internal hemorrhage no one else could see. I couldn't remember a single night I hadn't cried since the first week we were married. Anger, tears, separation. The ditch was getting wider. We moved farther apart, and he didn't even know it. What was worse, he didn't care. And in the end, I didn't either.

What had happened? How could this have turned out so wrong? I couldn't even pray. Was I really worthless? Again, that still, small voice, "No, you are worth so much more."

A year later, we bought our first home. He was still in seminary but was now the pastor of a small church, full of people who were excited to have a young preacher who could bring revival to their congregation and community. I held on to hope as our surroundings changed. I refused to stop believing for healing in our marriage. Ministering to others in a church where he was excited to pastor had to be a path to restoration.

Then one afternoon, I answered the phone at work. Anxiety ate away at my insides as I heard his raised voice. A list of my mistakes followed, ending with, "You can't do anything right."

Buried deep inside, I knew he was unreasonable, but why couldn't I do anything to please him? He let me know I had failed again. Would I ever be good enough? Maybe I was worthless. Once again, that still, small voice: "No, you are worth so much more."

Had it only been a few years since a bottle of Sprite crushed my flowers and my dreams began to die? I drove home after a long day at work, torn between praying his car would be in the driveway and praying he wouldn't be home.

The butterflies had left long ago. My stomach curled into a knot as I rounded the corner into our neighborhood. The driveway was empty. A mixture of relief and sadness tore me apart. I couldn't do this anymore.

Divorce. That word evokes such emotion. While some may throw it around without a thought, to me, it meant failure. It meant I couldn't fix it. It meant the end of a dream I believed was from God.

So how do we handle life when it doesn't turn out the way we expect? This is the question all of us must answer at some point in our lives. Our expectations, right or wrong, are many times what cause life's disappointments. But that is not a sign of failure.

At my lowest point, feeling I couldn't go on, I fell to my knees one night in my living room and poured out my heart to God. I told Him I couldn't live this way anymore; I couldn't keep going, and I told Him how scared I was. I turned to God with a desire to please Him versus wanting to please others by being the perfect wife and having the perfect home. I told Him how worthless I felt.

God enveloped me with a peace I couldn't understand but needed so much. He reminded me of His faith, His strength, His love, His peace, and His hope. He reminded me I was worth so much more because I was His precious child. By turning to God and His Word instilled in me through a Christian home, faithful leaders at my church, and study of Scripture, I survived and even blossomed.

After the divorce, I was tempted to wonder if I could still serve. I came to realize I didn't have to be a pastor's wife to serve Him. I could step out on my own and embrace His calling for me. God gave me gifts, and He didn't take them away because of divorce. Today, service looks different. It's writing, speaking, and hospitality. From early positions of supporting roles to now, having learned from great mentors on leadership and business, I'm preparing for my next season of life. Our gifts remain, but our service changes in different seasons.

God has richly blessed me. When divorce shattered my dreams, I turned to Christ and stopped trying to do it on my own. I could never be the perfect wife, the perfect pastor's wife, the perfect housekeeper, the perfect employee, the perfect mom, the perfect cook, the perfect author, the perfect speaker, the perfect anything. And I still can't. Perfection is no longer my goal. God's plan for me starts with pleasing Him in the roles He provides.

I look back now and see God's hand in ways I didn't then. He provided a job during the trials of marriage with supportive Christian leadership. When I felt like a failure at home, I survived because I felt valued at work. My life was worth something more.

Abuse in many forms ended my marriage. Not a definition of success by some people's standards. Yet, because of God's faithfulness, I'm not trapped in depression or guilt or the pain of my past. I am valued because God said I am worth so much more. My victory over the past was not only *setting* the foundation of His word when I was younger, but it came after I stepped out of the shelter of a Christian home and into the real world, requiring that I *stand* on that foundation.

You may not have had a scriptural grounding as a child, but you can start wherever you are. The days will pass whether or not we do anything with them. Think about where you will be five years from today, one year from today, six months from today, next month, next week, tomorrow. What will you do today to make a difference tomorrow?

Has God's Plan A for your life been messed up? Do you need Plan B, or maybe C, or D, or even Q or Z?

An empty space exists within each of us. We try to fill this space with material possessions, accomplishments, education, and the love of others. But this space was not designed for man-made trophies or emotions. It was not designed for love from a parent or spouse or child. It was not designed for anything that can change or fail. It was designed for the unchanging, unfailing love of One.

"God is love. In this the love of God was manifested toward us, that God has sent His only begotten Son into the world, that we might live through Him. In this is love, not that we loved God, but that He loved us and sent His Son to be the propitiation for our sins" (1 John 4:8–10 NKJV).

My life has moved through different seasons since that time. I have a job that is considered successful in the world's eyes. But this job doesn't define me. My worth is found in Christ alone because of His love, grace, and mercy. Every gift is from Him, and I will continue to walk forward in what He asks me to with those gifts.

Ephesians 2:10 (NKJV)

For we are His workmanship, created in Christ Jesus for good works, which God prepared beforehand that we should walk in them.

DONNA NABORS is a planner and organizer who has learned to trust God when things don't follow her plan. She speaks on transformation and has written several books pointing women to the truth in God's Word, including *Shattered Dreams to Treasured Truths*, where she shares about her first major life struggle. She believes that truth alone can bring us through our disappointments and trials.

Donna is a native Texan who loves cooking, baking, antiquing, and hospitality.

Connect with Donna on her website at donnanabors.com.

CHAPTER 11

The Lie in the Mirror

"IF YOU WANT TO be booked as a speaker, the smaller you are, the more likely you are to get speaking engagements." I listened in horror as a seasoned coach shared that plus-size women don't fit the ideal image, and my heart shrank while my body stayed the same. In that moment, I believed the lie that my worth and my calling were conditional on the weight I carried, as if shedding pounds were a prerequisite for being used by God. That false belief became a heavy burden, pushing me to strive instead of surrender.

It was as if someone had held up a mirror, not the kind that reflects your face, but the kind that distorts your worth. In that moment, I didn't see a woman called by God. I saw a woman who didn't measure up. The mirror didn't show my faith, my passion, or my purpose. It only magnified my size and whispered that it was too much. And I believed it.

My calling was crystal clear. Help hurting women heal. Show them how pain can be transformed into growth. Remind them they're not defined by the worst thing that happened to them, but by the One Who redeems all things. I knew it. I believed it. I taught it.

Until I didn't.

One comment from a coach, just one, landed like a brick in my gut. "The smaller you are, the more likely you are to get booked." Suddenly, my calling felt conditional. Like God had a weight requirement I'd missed in the fine print. I pictured God up in heaven, rubbing His temples like, "Bless her heart, she's still trying to squeeze into someone else's idea of calling." Maybe He had a clipboard, maybe not, but in my mind, He was gently shaking His head, whispering, "She's got plenty of faith, but apparently not the right dress size." As if my spiritual resume needed a weight-loss addendum before He could stamp it "approved."

So, I did what any determined, slightly panicked woman would do: I signed up for a medical fast. It sounded holy enough. Fasting is biblical, right? Esther fasted and saved a nation. Jesus fasted and launched His ministry. I figured I'd fast and finally fit into my calling ... and maybe my jeans.

The program came with weekly group therapy, which felt less like a sacred circle and more like storytelling hours. Everyone sharing their journey like chapters from a self-help memoir, hoping this time the ending will be different. One woman introduced herself with the kind of weary pride that comes from surviving battle. "I'm Sally. This is my second time. Lost ninety pounds, gained it back. Trying again."

I smiled politely, but inside I was thinking, "Not me. I'm not coming back." I was determined; this weight was going down, and my calling was going up. I'd lose it once and for all and ride off into my purpose like a triumphant Deborah, Israel's only female judge. Surely, she checked every box, right? Courage, wisdom, and let's be honest, a tunic that fit just right. In my mind, she was battle ready and body approved. If God could use her, maybe He'd use me too ... once I looked the part. And I did. For a while.

Over 100 pounds gone. Eight years of compliments, smaller dress sizes, and the sweet satisfaction of proving I could do it. I nodded politely when people asked how, but inside I was smug. *Not me. I'm a one-and-done kind of girl. I'll lose it, lock it, and throw away the key.* I floated through church lobbies like a walking before-and-after photo, convinced I had finally earned my place in God's spotlight.

But then life happened.

Stress crept in like a thief. Emotional eating tiptoed back in wearing a disguise, comfort food dressed up as self-care. And the weight returned like an uninvited guest who knew exactly where I kept the spare key.

Then came the moment.

I was walking into church, Bible in hand, heart ready to worship. And there she was, the greeter with the spiritual gift of unsolicited commentary.

"What's happening to you? You're getting bigger again!"

I froze. Smile plastered on. Heart plummeting. I wanted to vanish from the church entryway and reappear in the sanctuary like Jesus did with His disciples. No doors, no explanations, just suddenly present. If He could bypass walls, surely, I could bypass awkward encounters. Her words weren't just rude, they were the confirmation of every fear I'd buried beneath protein shakes and prayer journals.

I wasn't a success story anymore. I was a cautionary tale.

And in that moment, the lies roared louder than the truth. *You're disqualified. You're a disappointment. You're too much—again.*

But somewhere in the rubble of shame, a whisper broke through. Not mine. Not hers. His.

"I never measured you by the scale. I measured you by surrender."

That whisper didn't just comfort me, it confronted me. It peeled back the layers of striving I'd wrapped around my calling and exposed the quiet lie I'd been living that God's power in me was somehow tied to the size of me.

I thought success in ministry came with a dress size. That if I could just shrink my body, I'd finally expand my impact. But the truth is, I was chasing approval dressed up as purpose. And when the compliments faded and the weight returned, I feared my calling had too.

But God never called me to be a before-and-after photo. He called me to be a vessel, cracked, imperfect, real, and surrendered.

In the silence after the greeter's comment, when shame tried to write the final chapter, God whispered a different story:

"But the Lord said to Samuel, 'Do not look at his appearance or at the height of his stature, because I have rejected him; for God sees not as man sees, for man looks at the outward appearance, but the Lord looks at the heart'" (1 Samuel 16:7 NASB1995).

That verse isn't just a comfort; it's a correction. It reminds me that God never asked me to fit the mold. He asked me to follow Him. And following Him doesn't require perfection; it requires surrender.

So now, when I feel the pressure to perform or the sting of judgment, I return to this truth:

My worth isn't measured by numbers on a scale, but by the depth of my yes to God.

I realized I'd been striving for perfection instead of resting in God's unconditional love. When I stopped focusing on my flaws and started looking in His Word, I discovered that I am His daughter, His treasure, and His masterpiece just as I am.

Letting go of my need to earn His approval freed me to obey His call regardless of my size or résumé. I stepped out of my comfort zone to share His message of hope with hurting women, and with each bold yes, more speaking opportunities came. Obedience taught me that God doesn't wait for us to be perfect before He uses us. He simply asks us to trust and obey.

But what about you, my sister?

Have you ever stood in front of a mirror, not just the one in your bathroom, but the one in your mind, and heard whispers that didn't come from God? Lies that glide in quietly, dressed like truth, convincing you that you're not enough. Not smart enough. Not spiritual enough. Not polished, prepared, or worthy enough to be used by Him.

Maybe they came from a comment someone made years ago. Or from a comparison scrolling through social media. Or maybe, like me, they showed up in a moment when you were already vulnerable, when you were trying to step into your calling, but shame pulled you back like a shadow.

I've been there. I wish I could be there with you, sitting beside you on the couch, handing you a tissue if the tears start to fall, or standing next to you as you face that mirror, gently brushing away the lies that try to cloud your reflection.

Not to fix you. Not to judge you. Just to remind you that you're not alone. That someone sees you, believes in you, and knows that God's love for you has never been tied to your size, your past, or your performance. Because the same God Who called me while I was still tangled in lies is calling you, too. Not once you've cleaned up, slimmed down, or figured it all out. But now. As you are.

My sister, take a moment. Breathe deep. You've read my story, now let's gently turn toward yours.

What lies have crept into your heart, disguised as truth? Maybe they sound like these:

• "I'm too broken to be used."

• "I need to be more polished, more perfect, more put together."

• "If I looked different, I'd be more effective."

• "God's calling must've skipped over me."

Now, hold those lies up to the mirror of Scripture. Let God's Word speak louder.

"For we are God's masterpiece. He has created us anew in Christ Jesus, so we can do the good things he planned for us long ago" (Ephesians 2:10 NLT).

"You have been set apart as holy to the Lord your God, and he has chosen you from all the nations of the earth to be his own special treasure" (Deuteronomy 14:2 NLT).

"But He said to me, 'My grace is sufficient for you, for power is perfected in weakness.' Therefore, I will most gladly boast all the more about my weaknesses, so that Christ's power may reside in me. So I take pleasure in weaknesses, insults, catastrophes, persecutions, and in pressures, because of Christ. For when I am weak, then I am strong" (2 Corinthians 12:9–10 HCSB).

These aren't just verses to memorize; they're mirrors to stand in front of. They reveal who you truly are in Christ, not who the world says you should be. So, before you move on, pause. Let these truths settle deep. Let them interrupt the lies. And now, let's take a brave step together.

I encourage you to write down one lie you've believed about your worth or calling. Then, beside it, write a truth from Scripture that replaces it. Let this be your holy reflection, where shame is traded for healing, and striving gives way to surrender. You don't have to earn your worth. You only need to receive it.

Just so you know, I'm still on the journey toward a healthier lifestyle, but not to earn God's approval or prove my worth. That part's already settled. I'm doing it because I want to be here for the long haul, living out my calling with energy, joy, and maybe even chasing future grandbabies around the yard someday. These days, the mirror I stand in front of reflects truth, not lies. And my prayer for you, dear sister, is that you'll let God do the same, replacing every lie with His love, and every doubt with His delight in you.

Galatians 1:10 (NIV)
Am I now trying to win the approval of human beings, or of God? Or am I trying to please people? If I were still trying to please people, I would not be a servant of Christ.

When DONNA SCOTT speaks, women lean in, not just to her words, but to the hope woven through them. A licensed marriage and family therapist for thirty-three years, she has walked with countless women through heartbreak, helping them transform emotional pain into purpose. Her book, *The Tapestry of Trauma*, invites readers into her own healing journey from childhood sexual abuse, proof that God doesn't waste pain. Whether she's leading a Bible study or speaking at a retreat, Donna's message is clear: Healing is possible, and you don't have to walk it alone. She lives in San Diego with Ron, her husband of thirty-eight years, and they celebrate their four adult children.

Connect with Donna on her website at donnascotttherapy.com.

Chapter 12

From Shame to Purpose

As the tears streamed down my cheeks and raced to create a soggy sector on my pillowcase, the silence was broken. Suddenly, I heard a still small voice in my mind; it was the kind of voice you needed to be silent to hear. No noise. No distractions. Just stillness. You know those moments in time that are so significant they are defined by a before and an after? This was one of those moments.

God spoke and created this before and after. I could never go back to the before. The before was the common; the after was the uncommon.

"You're seeking validation from flawed humans instead of me," came the whisper.

My silent tears ceased, and my mind inexplicably calmed, creating a serene setting as I pondered what God had said. As I thought about what He said to me, I began to see the truth. I was going to others with my God-given giftings and asking them if they thought I was "on the right track" or if something was "good enough." Even worse? These people were distracting me from my purpose!

I was placing my divine purpose into the flawed hands of the fallen rather than trusting the promises of God.

After all, much like young David, who wouldn't deem me "unworthy" after hearing my life story? Heck! I'd deemed myself unworthy decades ago. I sold myself short, criticized my mistakes, and told myself I was unqualified because of my background.

And much like David, it was time to face my giants.

I stared at the document in my hand that confirmed my marriage was over. *Divorced.*

The overwhelming discomfort made me feel as though I couldn't take another step. *Weak.*

The pain of hearing some variation that I wasn't good enough repeatedly from multiple people. *Unwanted.*

The loneliness of sitting alone when my world fell apart. *Unloved.*

Seeing the scale light up at its highest point: 297. *Overweight.*

Seeing the scale numbers bounce from an all-time high to their lowest in years and then back up. *Overweight. Again.*

The apprehension of walking into that conference room and seeing HR at the table. *Unemployed.*

The paralyzing feeling of overwhelm, staring at a list of unfinished tasks begging for my attention. *Lazy.*

A mind swirling so rapidly that nothing made sense. *ADHD.*

All of these scenarios pointed to one unacceptable yet certain destination in the eyes of the world: *failure.*

But God wasn't done with me yet. Despite how I felt, He was there beside me in every one of these situations, but when I was leaning on my own strength, I didn't even think to ask Him for His strength. While I saw my weakness as a detriment, God saw it as an opportunity to lead me closer to Him and display His glory. What felt like failure in the moment was a chance for God to redeem and restore.

If failure is the opposite of success, let's look at how the world defines success. Oxford defines success as "the accomplishment of an aim or purpose."

Purpose.

It's no coincidence that success focuses on purpose when God created each of us with a divine purpose; obedience toward His divine purpose is the ultimate success, regardless of the world's opinions. God defines success differently than Oxford.

It's the willingness to say yes when your voice shakes. It's the ability to take a step when your legs threaten to collapse. It's sitting in silence, learning, rebuking, and healing. Clawing out from under the weighty expectations and goals placed upon you by others. Exchanging your plans for His. Embracing the uncommon life over a common life.

Learning to trust God consists of whispers, tears, wrestling with contradictions, and processing. Quite simply, learning to trust God is the act of surrender. It's dying to self. It's picking up your cross. It's turning to Jesus when you want to turn to the world. It's knowing that you will hear when it's all done: "Well done, my good and faithful servant" (Matthew 25:21 ESV).

Success is a life journey culminated only when we meet Jesus. In the here and now, success looks like seeking His face and His plans over my own.

In another parallel to David, I've also struggled with anger, temptation, jealousy, and my sinful nature. I have forgotten to pray and read my Bible. I have been distracted from my divine purpose. The world would deem me a failure, but there is no condemnation for those in Christ (Romans 8:1). Each of these failures, let alone the whole value-sized bundle, is a failure in the eyes of man, but God doesn't demand perfection as the world does.

Since I couldn't be trusted to navigate my own way to success, I spent my entire life chasing the approval of man. Putting my own ideas—ideas God had gifted me—on hold because someone somewhere "knew better." Squashing my need to discuss things that mattered because it made others uncomfortable. Agreeing with others because I had deemed *them* worthy. Allowing others to dissuade me from my assignment because I didn't feel as though I had any value to add. I had placed my worth and my calling in the hands of others for them to decide whether I was worthy.

I needed approval or validation for every task God asked me to do. Even a simple blog post meant asking multiple people if they thought the post was okay, rather than trusting that God was delivering a message through me. Many posts went unpublished, and messages went undelivered because someone didn't approve my message.

I desperately needed to know I was on the right track or if I had heard God correctly, as though others' opinions could provide definitive answers to those questions. Quite simply, I didn't trust myself enough to understand how to trust God. He had given me everything I needed, and still I doubted. How could this assignment be for me? Why would He entrust me with a message? How could God trust me to deliver on His plan? Doesn't He know who He is dealing with?

For most of my life, I was a stand-in, a nameless background character. Just as Jesse referred to David without name (Samuel 16:11) immediately before his anointing, I was often referred to by my failures (the fat one, the loud one, the ugly one). But God called me by my gifts. He saw in me what others couldn't. He saw the qualities He had placed inside me when He knit me together so carefully in my mother's womb (Psalm 139:13).

Growing up, I was the butt of unlimited jokes in school. Horrible and hurtful nicknames became my identity to my peers and to me. I was pushed on stairs, shamed for any attempt at relevance, and ridiculed relentlessly by people who deemed themselves judge and jury. I was nothing beyond my nicknames, someone "less than," who deserved whatever punishment the elite of the schoolyard decided to dish out that day. As a firefighter's kid, the youngsters I played with on the weekends at events became my tormentors in school. The juxtaposition between weekend and weekday was brutal.

On the other hand, I excelled academically in school. I was a perfectionist, unhappy with anything less than a perfect score. I pushed myself to do better. To be better. Anything less than a perfect score equated to failure in my mind. The words I spoke over myself were caustic and left scars, even more than the words others spoke over me.

In all relationships, my quest for perfectionism derailed any grace I may have had for myself. Perfection meant that I mattered in some way. My mind had already formed the opinion that anything less than perfect was a heinous grievance, so I was ruthless with myself. Unfortunately, I gravitated toward friends and others who shared my low opinion of myself.

There have been many along the way who have been happy to let me know that I don't matter, but their opinions (and mine) are no match for God's truth. The truth is this: We are all God's children, created with purpose on purpose for a divine purpose.

Even when I couldn't see past my own self-assessment, He never considered me a failure. Despite my unwillingness, disobedience, stubbornness, doubts, and struggles, He never removed the calling He placed on me before I ever breathed air. And He has never removed the calling He has placed on you, my friend.

God created each of us with intentionality.

God has always had a different plan from the world, along with a different scale for success. In His plan, everything meant to harm would fail (Isaiah 54:17) and all things meant for evil would be redeemed for good (Romans 8:28).

Over the past several years, I have partnered with God to heal the deep wounds I've accumulated over the decades from trying to live up to the world's idea of success. He has stepped in where others have left. He has held me close when I walked away. He has restored and redeemed parts of me I believed were lost forever.

It's been a tough and exhausting journey, and I am still in the middle of it, but it's been a path He led me to take. He has reminded me of the things He has called me to do, and He is equipping me despite my past. Well, "equipping" gives me far too much credit; He's pulling me closer to Him and lending me His strength.

My quest for answers about why people treated me horribly has faded into the landscape. I will never understand, but He has taught me how to forgive.

My inability to trust because of bitter betrayals has turned into an eagerness to trust Him.

My mean-girl mentality toward myself has turned into grace for my shortcomings.

I'm not perfect. I still battle these things daily. It's a constant recalibration, and some days it's more than I can handle.

But it's progress.

I am still learning what it means to trust. But God is patient, and He has a plan. He is the God Who sees (Genesis 16:13). He calls us to be still and understand who He is (Psalm 46:10). When we align our actions to His will, we succeed.

Sweet friend, if you are like me and have allowed the world to tell you who you are, take a moment and talk to the One Who has already defined you. Ask Him who you are. When the voices of the world become deafening, seek clarity from Him.

> Psalm 139:13–14 (ESV)
> For you formed my inward parts; you knitted me together in my mother's womb. I praise you, for I am fearfully and wonderfully made. Wonderful are your works; my soul knows it very well.

STEPHANIE WEBER is a mom to grown kids, a grandma, an almost-empty-nester, and a dutiful human to three quirky rescue pets. An Ohio-born (O-H!) author, speaker, and reseller, she's an IT pro by day and live-selling show host by night. A domestic abuse survivor who's wrestled with impostor syndrome and ADHD, Stef is finally rediscovering her creativity that was buried under years of self-doubt. Stephanie collects "But-God!" moments, forgets what she's doing mid-task, and picks up new hobbies like it's a sport (and she's the gold-medal winner!). Whether she's painting, writing, reading, or making a joyful mess in the kitchen, she finds peace in chaos. She loves Jesus, her Buckeyes, and reminding others of their identity in Christ—while learning to embrace her own, even when it's uncomfortable.

Connect with Stephanie on her website at stephanierweber.com.

CHAPTER 13

Beyond the Scale

MOST OF MY LIFE, Satan used two sharp weapons—jealousy and comparison—to keep me from walking in the destiny Christ prepared for me. Layer upon layer of trauma shaped my childhood, and food became my way of coping.

Being overweight often meant being labeled as "less than, lazy, and undisciplined." Those words and perceptions became deeply ingrained in my mind. Childhood trauma came in waves, some all at once, others years apart, but together they built a wall of shame. Every extra pound became a reminder of the pain I tried to bury.

In time, I began to believe a lie that settled deep in my soul and became a core belief: *I am a failure.*

In high school, the popular boys gave me a nickname related to my weight that still lingers in the back of my mind. Almost fifty years later, it is still so strong that I cannot even share the word. It's not an ugly word. It's simply a normal word used in a derogatory manner.

As an adult, I wondered how I could step into my calling and pursue what I believed God had placed in my heart if I was convinced I was already defeated. I rationalized that everyone else saw me the same way: lazy, undisciplined, and unworthy. I compared myself to society's definition of success: thin, beautiful, polished. Ironically, when I look back at pictures of my younger self, I see someone strong, healthy, and not overweight at all. But in the mirror, I only saw failure.

One night, after giving up on yet another diet, I fell to my knees, face soaked in tears, and cried out, "God, why haven't You changed my willpower? Why do I still look like this? How can You use me when I don't even feel comfortable in my own skin?"

I wasn't expecting an answer. I was lamenting. But, in His tenderness, God spoke to my heart. "You can reach people others cannot. I created you for a purpose. Your weight is not who you are."

It was never about the number on the scale. It was always about the calling. About the women who had cried the same tears and believed the same lies. And God whispered, "I chose you to reach them."

I had read 1 Samuel 16:7 countless times. "The Lord doesn't see things the way you see them. People judge by outward appearance, but the Lord looks at the heart" (NLT). For the first time, I came to understand that truth personally.

God also spoke these words over me: "You are worthy. You are loved. You have purpose."

It took years to believe, but slowly, my identity began to shift. My worth was no longer tied to what society calls success but to who I am in Christ. To me, true success is found in a pure heart before God.

The struggle didn't vanish overnight. I still fight the enemy's whispers, but today I remind him of who I am. I am God's workmanship, created in Christ Jesus for good works (Ephesians 2:10, my paraphrase). I am not my weight. I am not my flaws. I am His and made perfect in Christ alone.

Another verse became my foundation. "Above all else, guard your heart, for everything you do flows from it (Proverbs 4:23 NIV). I even wrote a book about guarding our hearts from Satan's lies. Because the truth is, Satan is clever, but we have victory in Jesus. Amen.

Jesus Himself said, "I came that they may have life, and may have it abundantly" (John 10:10 ESV). God spoke to me again and revealed that to live abundantly means to walk in the Fruit of the Spirit—love, joy, peace, patience, kindness, goodness, faithfulness, gentleness, and self-control (Galatians 5:22).

My story begins in my early years. While I should have been enjoying a carefree childhood, my mother suffered a nervous breakdown after my sister was born. My strongest memories are of her in the hospital or confined to her bed at home. Through the struggle, I watched God slowly heal her. Later, people meeting her couldn't believe she once battled crippling agoraphobia. I knew it was only by faith and God's restoring power that she was totally healed.

My father, carrying his issues, expressed them in anger and distance. I longed for his approval, but it rarely came. I can only recall once, at twenty-eight years old, when I felt he was proud of me, although he never said the words. Later in life, softened by God's grace, he even apologized. That, too, was the work of God.

During those fragile years, I carried responsibilities too heavy for a child—laundry, cooking, and caring for my younger siblings. When my parents couldn't meet our needs, others stepped in. However, one of those trusted to care for us became my abuser. The repeated violation had buried shame so deep that I tried to hide behind food, building what I thought was a protective shield around my childlike body.

As a teenager, I was exhausted by my striving, always trying to prove I was "enough." Striving for perfectionism became my stronghold. I longed for joy but didn't know where to find it.

In counseling years later, I described myself as a crumpled brown paper bag, discarded and worthless. But that's not why Jesus came. He endured the cross to declare that I am priceless. Scripture says, "You were bought with a price" (1 Corinthians 6:20 ESV). That price was His very life.

The value of something is determined by what someone is willing to pay for it, and Jesus paid it all for me and for you.

Today, I no longer see myself as a worthless paper bag. I am heavier today than at any time in the past, and I'm thankful God cares much more about the condition of my heart than the number on the scale.

Sweet sister, you are loved and adored by the same God Who created the universe, and He doesn't make junk!

Speaking of that worthless paper bag, God, through His relentless love, allows me to see myself as a sparkling gift bag, overflowing with His grace, and carrying His healing to others. Friend, He can do the same for you. I encourage you to cling to the Scriptures mentioned here or find ones that God has chosen to speak to you.

When I feel inadequate, I think of Acts 4:13, where ordinary, uneducated men were recognized as courageous because they had been with Jesus. This is how I want others to see me: just as I am, uneducated and ordinary. However, I also want them to realize that my radiant joy and hope stem from the time I've spent with Jesus and the love He has poured into my heart.

And when I doubt God's ability to use me, I remember Abraham. Hebrews 11:12 (NIV) says that "from this one man, and he as good as dead, came descendants as numerous as the stars." If God can use a man who was as good as dead to bear descendants as numerous as the stars, what can He do with a generation of women who are surrendered to Him and find their success in obedience to Him?

God delights in using the unlikely, the broken, the overlooked. That means there is hope for all of us.

Psalm 139:14 (NIV) I praise you because I am fearfully and wonderfully made; your works are wonderful, I know that full well.

TRISH KUHL is an inspirational Christian author, speaker, and founder of *Living in Abundance*, a ministry devoted to helping women embrace the abundant life God promises through Jesus Christ.

Having once struggled with feelings of inadequacy, Trish encountered the redeeming love of Christ and discovered freedom, healing, and purpose in Him. Her heart is to help women know they are deeply loved, worthy, and created with purpose.

She shares her message through writing, speaking, and retreats that encourage women to walk boldly in their God-given identity and calling. In addition, Trish has coauthored *Jingle Your Jolly* and is currently working on *Jingle Your Jolly, the Grandma Way*, with Joy Michele Chitsey. She is also the author of *Living in Abundance: Exploring Your Worth, The Depth of God's Love, and His Purpose for You*.

Trish enjoys painting, photography, volunteering, and spending time outdoors. Her greatest joy is being "Mimi" to her beloved grandson, Isaiah.

Connect with Trish on her website at TrishKuhl.com.

Chapter 14

Exchanging Lies for Truth

DIAPERS, DISHES, AND TOYS cluttered my home, despite my best intentions to get my act together. Little kids ran around in need of attention. For the first time in many years, my brother was paying me a voluntary solo visit. His work had him passing through our dusty out-of-the-way town, and I was excited to see him.

Only eighteen months apart, my little brother and I had once been very close. As kids, we shared games, friends, adventures, and a mutual love for Jesus. But now my brother was a successful, middle-aged, good-looking attorney with commanding communication skills. He dressed in expensive professional clothes and had his own growing law firm and a trendy post-modern worldview I didn't understand and dared not question. And me? I felt sloppy with uncovered gray roots, surrounded by diaper-clad babies, piles of laundry, student loan debt, and walls cluttered with dated Hobby Lobby signage.

I don't remember my brother's visit that day. I just remember how I felt afterwards.

I felt like a failure. I knew I wasn't one. But nevertheless, the feeling washed over me.

This world worships status. Money. Material possessions. A powerful reputation. Everything my brother had was attractive, and I knew it because I liked those things too. I know success in God's kingdom is about surrender and obedience. The problem is God's kingdom isn't always front and center in my mind.

As a young girl, I dreamed of becoming an author, magazine journalist, or actress in New York City. I spent hours creating stories, and I hoped I would one day make a name for myself. After earning my millions in New York City, I planned to settle down on the East Coast in a tree-lined white Georgian style mansion with a pool and guest house, marry a tall, dark, and handsome hottie (who I imagined was an exact replica of Hollywood golden age star Cary Grant), have four grown children with that man, and tour the world via train and luxury boats. I had what some would call a vivid imagination. But trust me when I say I had it all mapped out.

Diapers, dishes, and laundry had never been part of my plan. In fact, in all my dreaming, I never imagined raising children. Not ever. My daydreams only included adult kids who appeared well-adjusted and fully potty-trained.

But God has a sense of humor. Or as I heard one speaker wisely say, God has a strategic sense of humor.

I dreamed of Manhattan. I got a husband from North Dakota with no desire for city living.

I dreamed of already-launched babies. I got the incredible opportunity to raise them.

I dreamed of fortune and fame. I got student loan debt and a town in the desert.

I dreamed of glamour and the perfect figure. I got early gray hairs and cellulite.

I dreamed of making a name for myself. I got a jealous God Who wanted my heart.

I dreamed of my way. Instead, I got His.

I didn't realize that surrender was the game plan when preschool me signed up to follow Jesus. I had already been a Christian for a few years when I was baptized at the age of seven. My mom especially had a deep love for Jesus and shared her love for the Word of God and about Jesus' gift of eternal life. Yes, of course I wanted Him!

And like my mother, I felt compelled to share about Christ with others. I remember as a little girl being on a metro bus field trip with my mom and younger brother. In my memory, everyone on that bus looked sad. I remember one man in particular who seemed lonely and depressed. I wanted to cheer him up, so I said, "Everyone here who loves Jesus, raise their hand!" Silence. So, I yelled louder, "Everyone here who loves Jesus, raise their hand!" I turned to my mother and asked, "Mommy, why is no one raising their hands?" As an adult, I look back knowing that probably wasn't the best way to share about Jesus. But it saddened me even at a very young age that someone would not know the eternal hope found in Him.

Yet for many years, I was the girl who loved Jesus, who knew the hope that Jesus promised, but also struggled to believe Him. I held onto a secret lie I believed about myself. For years, I quietly lived in rejection. My family of origin is complicated, with several family members dealing with their own wounds of abandonment. I was sensitive to loved ones who were in and out of my life, and I felt like a throwaway person.

It's one thing to feel the sting of something. It's another to accept a feeling as truth. And it's another to accept a lie as your identity. Somewhere along the line, my feeling of being a throwaway person became a full-grown belief. Despite wanting Jesus, my childhood was filled with a longing for acceptance and love that I couldn't quite find. I was on a quest that had me looking for fulfillment in other places.

Someone who labels herself a throwaway person believes she needs to prove to the world that she's otherwise. Only, no amount of human relationships, applauded stories, writing awards, career opportunities, degrees, or world travels could satisfy the deep desire I had to be accepted and loved.

I thought that my secret lie was only about me. I thought my lie was solely about my identity. But it really was about God. It was about His identity. Because what I believed about being a throwaway was my refusing to believe Him.

His Word says His children are:

- Image bearers (Genesis 1:27)
- Created with intentionality (Psalm 139:14)
- Chosen (Colossians 3:12)
- Loved (1 John 4:10)
- Forgiven (1 John 1:9)
- Purpose-full (Ephesians 2:10)
- Special (1 Peter 2:9)
- Accepted (Ephesians 3:12)

In John 10:10 (NIV), Jesus says, "The thief comes only to steal and kill and destroy; I have come that they may have life, and have it to the full."

It turns out the lying thief has an agenda. Lies—especially lies about identity—have consequences. They are designed to steal purpose, kill joy, and destroy our relationship with our Maker. The lies made me believe I had to accomplish something, do something, make a name for myself. But Jesus said He came so I might have life and have it abundantly.

It took many years for me to realize:

If I believe I'm an image bearer, I know I have tremendous worth because of my Maker. I want to know Him.

If I believe I am chosen, I know that God cares for me. No matter what my circumstances, He won't leave me or forsake me.

If I believe I am loved, I know that God the Father sacrificed His one and only Son for me. I matter to Him.

If I believe I am purpose-full, I know that no matter what I go through, no matter what my capacities or limitations are, my life has meaning. Despite what the world says about doing more to be successful, God says I can trust Him. He's done all the work. Now I just rest in Him.

If I believe I am accepted, I know that no matter how many times I mess up, I can still come to the Lord. God is never going to reject me when I reach out to Him.

I spent a lot of time ignoring what the Bible says and instead trying to find something that would validate me. In many ways, I was ignorant of the deception. I never stopped to think, "What lie am I believing?" But in my late twenties, I had a faith crisis.

God wasn't showing up the way I thought He should. I thought I had done my part, why hadn't He done His? Was He even there? I didn't realize how small the Creator of the Universe had become in my mind. My failings had become so big, and all the things I had tried to find fulfillment in other than Jesus were falling short. My career at the time was great but exhausting. My husband was loving but imperfect. Luxuries were expensive, and travel caused anxiety. And attempts to have a family were painful—my husband and I had suffered multiple miscarriages.

I was invited to a Bible study that was about believing in God. As I studied the Bible and the character of God, I began to realize I was dismissing and ignoring what God says about Himself and what He says about His children. I was choosing to believe circumstantial feelings more than the unchanging truth. I was choosing to worship a poor shadow of who He really is, instead of surrendering to Him.

James 4:7–10 (NIV) says, "Submit yourselves, then, to God. Resist the devil, and he will flee from you. Come near to God and He will come near to you. Wash your hands, you sinners, and purify your hearts, you double-minded. Grieve, mourn and wail. Change your laughter to mourning and your joy to gloom. Humble yourselves before the Lord, and He will lift you up."

By the time I really wanted the Lord for who He is, not for what He could do for my dreams, I had believed not just one lie but many. I had to repent of the lies I had believed. But God is gracious. He meets us where we're at when we simply come.

My circumstances left me feeling like I was a throwaway person. My God said something else. In that moment of crisis, I had to decide. Who was I going to follow?

I told Jesus I was going with Him.

I've found it's not about my circumstances so much as it's about simply listening to Jesus. Jesus said His sheep hear His voice, and they will not follow the voice of another because they don't recognize him (John 10).

Fast forward to marrying that North Dakotan man, raising four kids, hosting exchange students who are like daughters from around the world, launching a podcast and speaking ministry. You know what? It turns out God writes the best stories.

Frankly, the thief still does his best on the regular to steal, kill, and destroy. There are triggering things for me even now. It could be feeling left out, perceiving a loved one's disappointment in my life choices, or comparing my success to someone else's. It could even be a reminder of unfulfilled dreams I thought I laid down years ago ...

And the devil whispers, "You're a throwaway person."

The day my brother visited me and I felt like a failure, I may have let the feeling sit for a bit. I was tempted to believe that old familiar lie.

But at some point, no matter what the circumstances or the feelings that come, I can choose to resist the lie. I can choose to remind myself of who my God is and what He says about me. I can reach out to a trusted friend and ask for prayer. When I resist the devil, I watch him flee. I've found that to be true, over and over again.

And then I have the choice to get up out of my pity party and remind myself that Jesus loves me, this I know. I continue one step at a time with the God I've learned to trust. By resting in His character, His timing, His goodness, His way, I am free. Maybe freedom looks like taking care of a huge pile of laundry that no one but God sees. Maybe freedom looks like telling the local coffee barista about the God Who loves her. Maybe freedom looks like talking about the realness of Jesus on my podcast or from a platform. Maybe one day I'll go to New York or travel the world. I won't rule anything out because only God knows. But the bottom line: Jesus loves me, this I know. I'm not a throwaway person. And I'm learning that being successful in His eyes is all about knowing His voice and following Him wherever He leads.

> John 10:27 (NIV)
>
> My sheep listen to my voice; I know them, and they follow me.

JANELL WOOD is a writer, speaker, and podcast host who loves sharing about Jesus Christ. She holds a master's degree in counseling psychology from Northwest University and has a background in advocacy and ministry, walking with women through conversations about doubt, identity, and hope. A graduate of the CrossExamined Instructor Academy, Janell is passionate about Christian apologetics and clarifying tough questions about God and purpose. As founder of *Finding Something REAL,* she creates space for young women to ask hard questions and models the importance of meeting people where they are. At home, she and her husband Brian are busy raising their four kids, welcoming international students, and chasing after two mischievous dogs—daily reminders that grace shines brightly in chaos!

Connect with Janell on her website at findingsomethingreal.com.

MOTHERHOOD

Chapter 15

Finding Purpose in the Hidden Places

HIDDEN.

That's the best way I can describe the last sixteen years of my life. Not invisible, not forgotten—just unseen. Quiet. Tucked behind the curtain of a busy life. A life filled with purpose, but with little applause.

You see, many years ago, I made the choice to homeschool my children. To help run our family business from behind the scenes. To build our home and life on our family farm nestled in the back of a cow pasture. None of these choices landed me in the spotlight of society. There are no trophies. No promotions. No awards or performance reviews.

And yet, each of these is a specific calling God asked of me.

One Sunday morning, as I sat in church, heavily pregnant with our first daughter, the pastor preached about how little time families get to spend with each other once the world's influences start to pull them apart. He said, according to research, it takes 10,000 hours of training for someone to become an expert in something. Suppose we add up the time families have to spend together after school, sports, and other activities pull them in different directions. In that case, there just isn't enough time left over to spend with our kids to help them become experts in the Christian faith, unless we become radically intentional.

I sat paralyzed with fear. As a new mom, how would I have the time to teach this sweet baby everything she needed to know about God, faith, and living for Christ before releasing her into this cruel world? It was these moments of doubt and questioning that God began to nudge my heart toward homeschooling. However, as a public school teacher and early childhood instructor, I was adamant that I would *never* homeschool. It felt too hard—too isolating. And didn't only crazy people homeschool their kids?

But God has a sense of humor.

One person after another entered my life—other mothers I watched from afar—homeschooling their children with grace and confidence. Then, when my dearest friend told me she was going to homeschool her children, I swallowed my pride, got real with God, and reluctantly prayed, "Lord, is this what you *really* want for our family?"

Still, I assumed (and secretly hoped) that my husband's answer would be a firm no. But one night at supper, he looked at me from across the table and said, "I think we need to try this homeschooling thing and see how it goes."

My mouth dropped open. Did he really just say *that*? My stomach tightened because I knew what this would mean. Homeschooling, while running a business and raising a young family, would require *everything* from me. So much of myself would need to be laid down at the foot of the cross—those dreams, my coveted free time, my career ambitions, and all the recognition that came with it. And I would have to eat my own words and become *that* crazy person.

Many years have passed living in this hidden place. I watched my peers earn awards, receive PhDs, write books, and climb the corporate ladder. I even wholeheartedly celebrated and cheered them on. Meanwhile, I changed countless diapers, taught phonics, and solved business crises behind the scenes. There were no medals for extinguishing business fires or calming toddler meltdowns. Just me often feeling exhausted, sometimes resentful, always pouring out.

But in motherhood, and in business ownership, there is this sacred kind of sacrifice that nobody applauds. We sow seeds that no one sees. Hidden—we pour out without much reward. We give, and give, and give again, with little sign of harvest.

But those buried seeds ... they're planted. And eventually, they do grow.

With a bit of time. A little water. Some sunshine. And a whole lot of love, grace, and prayer. Slowly, the tiny buds of fruit begin to appear.

Now, I'm nearly seventeen years into this motherhood journey and am finally beginning to see a small harvest after many years of labor. My children are growing into people I deeply admire. And after fifteen years of running a business with my husband, we finally live less time in crisis control. Thankfully, most days we can breathe. The wisdom gained from surviving many fires over the years now helps us put them out quickly.

And after believing God was finished growing our family, our family just welcomed a sweet surprise baby in our forties. Did I ever think that I would be this age, starting over, raising a baby? No way! I feel old. And yep, a lot of people have told me I'm crazy. But I have seen the overwhelming hand of God in how deeply my older daughters adore their baby sister. I also now know how fleeting these tiny years fly by. And I welcome with an open heart this precious gift from above, which I never thought I would get to experience again.

Am I still hidden? Yes, but I no longer resent it (at least not on most days).

I've come to embrace that *hidden doesn't mean forgotten*.

God sees.

He sees every diaper changed, every lesson taught, every tear wiped off chubby little cheeks. He even tenderly holds and counts the tears we as mothers cry in secret. He sees me when no one else does. And He meets my every need, often in ways I don't even think to ask for.

There are days I still struggle. When I start to feel like I haven't accomplished enough. When the voice of comparison creeps in, usually through social media, and tells me I should be doing more. Should *be* more. But when Satan's comparison trap starts lurking around the hidden corners of my thoughts, I must stop them and remind myself that God doesn't ask me to measure my calling by someone else's. He simply asks me to obey. I don't want to be like the people Jesus warned us about in John 12:43 (NIV), who "loved human praise more than praise from God."

When I start craving the world's approval, I have to stop my unhealthy thinking and ask myself, "Who am I serving? God or man?"

When schooling my kids feels too hard, "Who am I serving?"

When I'm ready to give up and quit everything because I don't think I can keep doing it all, "Who am I serving?"

When life continually throws its unrelenting curve balls, "Who am I serving?"

It's a question I come back to daily because my pride often tries to speak louder than my purpose. And yet, my purpose to serve my family is clear.

Matthew 16:25 (NIV) tells us, "Whoever wants to save their life will lose it, but whoever loses their life for me will find it." Laying my life down for a season doesn't mean I'm giving up on my own God-given dreams. He still has divinely planted beautiful desires in my heart that haven't yet come to life—and that's okay. His timing is best. But also, over the years, the dreams I once had no longer seem so important. It's like God has grafted His desires in my heart over the frivolous things I once thought I needed.

Culture says self-sacrifice is outdated. That motherhood gets in the way of self-care. But the Bible says in John 15:13 (ESV), Jesus "lay down his life for His friends." If we're called to reflect His light and love, we must embrace sacrifice, not because it's easy, but because in it we find true soul care.

Soul care goes deeper than bubble baths and coffee breaks. It looks like soaking in God's Word, watching beauty bloom in a backyard garden, surrounding ourselves with Christian friends who lift us up, and trusting that the seeds we plant in our children's hearts and in the lives of others around us will grow into the eternal fruit of salvation.

The media-driven world around us doesn't want us to see these beautiful gifts from God. Instead, it shows us highlight reels. Endless world disasters. Filtered videos of "perfect" influencers. Glittery advertisements enticing us to buy the next thing to fix all our problems, while simultaneously telling us we're not good enough as we are.

But, in our quietest moments, God is always there. Always gently nudging us along and whispering to our hearts that we are enough to Him, even when we feel forgotten or overlooked. And it's during these seemingly hidden times that we can often sense His comforting presence the clearest. I trust that God still isn't finished with us. His story and purposes are still unfolding in each of our lives. "And we know that for those who love God all things work together for good, for those who are called according to his purpose" Romans 8:28 (ESV). So, let's hold on tight to this promise, for it reminds us that every challenge, every heartache, and every moment of self-doubt and uncertainty leads us toward a future filled with hope and purpose. Our purpose is defined not by who the world says we should be or what we should do, but by our heavenly Father, Who cares so deeply for us.

It's so easy for us to measure our success and even our worth by the world's standards. We look at how much we accomplish, how productive we are, how much money we've made, or how impressive our life might look to others.

But a wise pastor once told me, "In God's economy, the way up is down."

Success might look like rocking a baby with tears in our eyes because we're so exhausted we can hardly keep them open. It might look like sitting at a table teaching math to our child when both of us would rather give up. Or it might even look like staying up late at night to listen to our teenager pour her heart out.

The world doesn't see these hidden, not-so-glamorous moments. But God does. He is present in them. And when we choose to be faithful in the ordinary, unseen places, He is faithful to stand beside us to guide and strengthen us.

At the end of this life, it won't matter how many awards we received, how productive we were each day, or how much wealth we accumulated. God doesn't measure success the way the world does. In His eyes, success is not about the number of social media followers, our influence, and recognition—it's about the posture of our hearts. He is looking for faithfulness, not flashiness. What will matter is whether we served Jesus with a sincere heart.

And one day, when this life ends and we take our first step into eternity, the only words that will truly matter will be the ones whispered by our Heavenly Father. "Well done, my child. My good and faithful servant." Because He is the only One Who is there with us through all our hidden moments—the ones that no one else sees. He's the One holding us up, guiding us, loving us, and cheering us on.

Matthew 16:25 (NIV)
Whoever wants to save their life will lose it,
but whoever loses their life for me will find it.

MACKI SMITH is a writer, business owner, and homeschooling mom to four energetic daughters. She and her family live on a farm in rural Mississippi with cows, horses, chickens, dogs, cats, and a fish named Bling. Before raising a family, Macki taught kindergarten and special education and led her church's women's ministry. Now, she spends her days helping her husband manage their veterinary practice while schooling her daughters and ministering to women along the way. She enjoys sharing stories through writing about faith, family, and farm life. As the adage goes, the days are long, and the years are short, so she's making the most of the years of having her little ones at home. On any given day, you may find her with a strong cup of coffee in hand, chasing the kids back into the house, the chickens back into their coop, or the cows back into the pasture.

Connect with Macki on her website at macki-smith.com.

CHAPTER 16

A Love that Changed a Generation

My grandfather died doing what he loved, planting his garden, with a pack of seeds still gripped in his fist. He wasn't a rich man. He wasn't famous. He was a simple man. He had a way of bringing me into his world like no one else could; he made me feel as if I were the only person in the world. Every year, I begged to go on vacation with my grandparents, and the answer was always yes. We made memories around sandcastles, salt air, and sandy feet.

Gardening was my grandfather's passion, and it showed when fresh vegetables were shared around our dinner table. I loved to follow him around his garden, his sacred place, where he explained how each plant was planted and nurtured. I still love to run my hands across a tomato plant to take in the scent that takes me back to that sacred place.

I was born to two young teenagers. Love brought me into this world, but a love that did not last. My mother remarried, and raising another man's child would not come easily for my new father. He provided for me in many ways my biological father did not. One father gave me his last name, and the other gave me life. My younger years were distant from both fathers, leaving me with a deep daddy wound. A wound I would try filling on my own for years to come. There is no such thing as a perfect parent, and because of God's goodness and faithfulness, He wastes nothing. Over time, God would bring me to a place where brokenness and love meet. He chose me by weaving a legacy of love into my life. A legacy of love that He is still weaving throughout my life today.

When I was a little girl, my grandfather gathered up my cousins and me around that old wooden piano bench to play hymns. He looked out over the top of his horn-rimmed glasses, sometimes singing his own version of "How Great Thou Art." I can still smell the pages of the old hymnal, and inside the cover, there is a stamp that reads "Holmes Street Methodist Church," the church my grandparents attended. I will never forget how they made me feel. In the presence of my grandfather, I felt seen and entirely accepted. Beside him was a safe place where I didn't have to earn his love.

My grandfather showed his love for Jesus through the way he loved my grandmother, just as Christ loved the church. The way he loved me. The way he prayed for me. The way he stood in the gap for me when I needed a daddy in my life. He had a certain boldness about him, the kind that was not afraid to share Jesus with anyone who crossed his path. He was the one man in my life who taught me about the love of Jesus. I was devastated when he left this earth, but because of the impact my grandfather made in my life, I knew God had more. The legacy of love was drawing me closer to Jesus.

In my teenage years, I occasionally attended church with a friend. I saw church as a place where there were more rules to follow outside of my home. But as a new wife, I wanted more, and God was giving me a hunger for Him.

"Turn to the book of Matthew," the pastor said from the pulpit. I clung to my *Precious Moments Bible* written in the King James Version. I thought somehow this Bible would replace all the children's Bible stories that were missing from my life. As I flipped through the pages, I thought, "Where is the book of Matthew?" But as the music played, I stood, the hymnal clutched to my chest, and tears streamed down my cheek.

It was a familiar song, one my heart knew. It felt like home. The words took my breath away as it began to play, "Oh Lord my God when I in awesome wonder, consider all the worlds Thy hands have made." Yes, it was the old familiar hymn, "How Great Thou Art." Church was an unfamiliar place for me, and I had no idea where the book of Matthew was in the Bible, but my heart knew the exact words to the old hymn. Memories flooded my soul as I remembered the last time I heard it.

It was just a few years earlier when it played at my grandfather's funeral. My connection to Jesus had left this earth, yet I could still hear his voice so vividly in my head. I prayed I would never forget what his hands looked like, and I closed my eyes to remember how they scrolled across the keys of the piano. The seeds in his garden were not the only seeds he planted. He left a legacy of love that lives within me. The pursuit of God's love for me, through my grandfather, planted the seed for a generational change for my family and beyond. I so desperately wanted the words within those pages of the Bible to come alive just as my grandfather talked about. I wanted my children, my family, and me to know this legacy of love that came only from knowing Jesus.

God laid down His foundation for me to walk on, and Psalm 23 came to life inside me. "Surely your goodness and love will follow me all the days of my life" (Psalm 23:6 NIV).

There was a time in my life when I thought success was built around what the world taught. A second income meant bigger, better, and nicer things, but staying home with my children was never a second thought. I thought my purpose needed to be more than "just a mom." Had I failed at life by not finishing college? Looking back over the years, what could I have done differently? These questions left me feeling like I was living out my purpose with minimal success. I fell into the trap of *what if* by thinking that if my plans were different, they might have been greater.

Proverbs 16:9 (NLT) says, "We can make our plans, but the Lord determines our steps."

Jesus became the light in my life by gently placing His hand on my back, even as a little girl, telling me to step onto a different path. God knew what my heart needed by making me a mother. Not a perfect mother. A mother who would guide a new generation by locking her eyes with Jesus. God gifted me the blessings of holding my children tight when tears were streaming, seeing every ball game and dance recital, being a room mom, watching every child drive away for the first time, snapping a gazillion pictures at prom, dropping them off at college, and now watching them step into parenthood. Motherhood was more than a title for me; it is my calling and my purpose. Mother Teresa said, "If you want to change the world, go home and love your family." And that's exactly what I did.

God makes all things new. Isaiah 43:18–19 (NLT) says, "But forget all that—it is nothing compared to what I am going to do. For I am about to do something new."

We all yearn for that place only Jesus can fill. He is a good Father Who created us with a plan and a purpose, even before we were born. He made us for more. There is hope and healing in the power of our God,

Who follows us all the days of our lives—reworking us, restoring us, and renewing us, covering us and teaching us and changing us for His purpose.

"For we are God's masterpiece. He has created us anew in Christ Jesus, so we can do the good things he planned for us long ago" (Ephesians 2:10 NLT).

I am a reminder of God's goodness and faithfulness. I was a broken little girl from a fractured family. A spirit of rejection blinded me. There was a time when I chose the world over Truth. I tried to disqualify myself from the life God chose for me. But it was the love of Jesus Who chose me, restored me, and used me by leaving His legacy of love to carry on to the next generation.

No matter what life brings to our table, God will complete the work He has for us. "And I am sure that God, who began the good work within you, will continue his work until it is finally finished on the day when Christ Jesus returns" (Philippians 1:6 NLT).

The seeds of my grandfather's heart were never wasted. They reached more than just me and my children. My whole family is restored to Jesus, even my relationship with my earthly father. Sundays are now spent side by side with Mom and Dad, worshiping Jesus. Only Jesus could sow a legacy of love that changed our hearts.

As I hold the hands of my grandchildren, God nudges me to leave a legacy of love inside their hearts. No matter what our past looks like, God wastes nothing.

The definition of the word hymn is a praise or celebration. I never learned to play the piano, but my hymn comes in different forms. Gently stroking my grandkids' soft hands, seeing their faces light up when they lock eyes with me, playing a game of Candy Land, having fun on our bear hunts in the woods, swinging at the park, and singing over them as I rock them to sleep—these are my hymns of praise.

What hymn will you sing? What seeds will you plant? Faith in Jesus becomes the foundation to leave a legacy of love for generations to follow.

Exodus 20:6 (NLT)

But I lavish unfailing love for a thousand generations
on those who love me and obey my commands.

MARY BETH POWERS carries the call to help other women build Christ-centered families, where faith becomes the foundation and leaves a legacy for generations to follow.

Mary Beth is a certified speaker, author, longtime Bible teacher, and serves as a connection pastor at her church. Whether sitting across the table from her or sitting with a room full of women, you will hear her powerful message. She speaks and writes with authenticity and truth, so women feel understood. Her smile, infectious personality, and a gift of hospitality invite people into her home and heart.

Spending time with family is a top priority for Mary Beth. She is married to her forever crush, Mike. Together, they raised three amazing children and live in North Alabama. They are enjoying the empty-nest season, and together, they love to travel and try out new restaurants.

She now carries a new favorite role as a Nana to her five grandchildren. She feels blessed to carry on a faith-filled generation.

Connect with Mary Beth on her website at marybethpowers.com.

Chapter 17

Favored and Forgiven

At the ripe old age of seventeen, I decided to marry the boy I'd been dating during the last couple of years of high school. Even as these words appear in print before my eyes, I can't help but notice the word "boy." I'm now sixty-seven years old and still refer to that moment as deciding to marry a boy. Who does that? Marries a boy?

My piano teacher, Bobbie, doubled as a mentor. There were so many people in town who wanted her as their piano instructor that she grouped them into classes of four students at a time. Her studio boasted four pianos. Most of her students learned pop songs of the day.

When I expressed my desire to focus on playing worship music, her schedule was full. Rather than saying she did not have room for another private student, she prayed. Then she acted on her prayer and sought permission from the school to exempt me one day a week from PE class. She took me to her house during the time slot for a piano lesson. Thinking back on her creative persistence to serve me as an individual, I'm amazed. She did not say, "There's not a time available." She said, "Let me pray and see what we can work out."

Bobbie also served as the accompanist at our church, a congregation averaging 2,000 people on Sunday mornings. She could sit at the keyboard and take your heart to a place of deep worship without ever singing a word. I wanted to play like her. I wanted to be like her. Her joyful spirit was contagious.

When I was sixteen, the church organist needed a three-month sabbatical. Bobbie mentored me to play for the church in her absence. How often does a sixteen-year-old receive an invitation to play for a worship service with that many attendees? God poured out His favor on me time and time again.

Because Bobbie held such a dear place in my heart, when she did not express excitement at my announcement, "I'm getting married," it hurt my feelings. "Can we go get a Coke after church?" I asked her, wanting to understand her disapproval. "I can tell you are not happy about my engagement, and I don't understand why." Part of me wanted to cry. The other part felt a little angry.

Bobbie chatted with me for a while, then she got to the point. "This man may be a Christian, but he does not love the Lord like you, Joni. It's going to cause you great pain." Her words stung because I knew she was right. While her life story was unknown to me, I did know that her current husband was not the father of her sons. That should have told me that she was speaking from experience.

Still, did I listen to her attempt to do what the Bible calls "iron sharpening iron"? No, I did not. I married that boy who caught my eye, knowing full well that his commitment to Jesus did not come close to matching mine. He had no intention of dwelling near to the heart of God and helping me do the same.

I let the world's definition of success direct my actions. My intended husband was good-looking, fun, and acquainted with people who seemed important to me. We bought our first house as seventeen-year-old kids. I left my mom and dad's home for a house of my own, not college, not an apartment, but for a house with my name on the title.

Was God right there with me while I ignored His guidance? Yes, every step of the way. Fast forward a few years.

My first baby arrived just after my twenty-first birthday. After a difficult labor and an emergency C-section, which turned into a womb infection, I was weak and ill. My parents took us to their house for a few days of recovery, then our little family settled in at our own home to heal and learn how to parent. I had left my house in perfect condition, thinking my hospital stay would be twenty-four hours. Two weeks later, when I finally got back home, I found myself trembling in the kitchen with my baby girl crying in the other room.

The kitchen surrounding me had no clean dishes, no groceries, and not one clean surface where I could even prepare a baby bottle. It was a new mom's nightmare. My husband moved his buddy in while I was in the hospital without even mentioning it to me. My heart screamed, "God, I can't do this!" The only voice louder than my despair was that of my baby. Her shrill cry shattered my composure.

In the same instant I cried for help, the Spirit of God living in me took my despair, calmed me, and helped me. These are not moments that you look back on in your faith story as proud moments. They don't look very victorious. They are the day-in and day-out challenges that make us question our relationship with God. I've learned that God's not rattled by things that seem to rock my world.

My marriage did not end at that moment. We continued to carry on as a family for another couple of years. See, God is patient with us. He was patient with both me and my husband. He loved us both amid our flawed choices.

When enough events had taken place that I felt my sanity suffering, I realized my daughter needed one stable parent. It would have to be me.

I woke up sick one morning, and the words, "Can you drop Crystal off at day care on your way to work?" sent my husband into a fury. "Never mind," I said. "I'll take care of it."

A phone call to Mom, who lived just a few blocks from me, helped me take a step I never wanted to take. "I don't know how to find an attorney. I need to file for a divorce."

Mom helped me get my daughter to day care and drove me to an attorney's office. The words coming from my mouth, "I need to file for a divorce," tasted horrible. However, when the assistant handed me paperwork to fill out, my heart paused. The words at the top of the paper said, "I Pray for Peace." Though I could not have put the thought together with words, that was exactly what I prayed for. God knew. Again, in the middle of consequences caused by my choice, He breathed possibility into my darkest moment. I was calm on what was probably the worst day of my life.

One of my biggest heartaches was the concept that my sweet little girl would not likely have a sibling close to her age. If it was years before I remarried, she would be like an only child. My own sisters were so important to me. I did not want to rob her of that type of close family relationship. Still, the next week, when I went to the doctor for a routine visit, shock grabbed me when the doctor announced that I was pregnant.

My feelings of joy and relief about the news baffled even me. I cried tears of joy as I drove away from that appointment. Was God listening to my heart cry out on behalf of my little girl for such an untimely request? My daughter would have a sibling close to her age. Delight and awe overcame me, knowing that God again granted my heart's desire. The sequence of events unfolding in my life made it clear that God understood me. He understood my heart.

In the coming weeks of waiting for the arrival of this new family member, I attended a divorce recovery workshop. To end each session, the leader asked participants to repeat this phrase: "I'm single. I'm divorced. I'm OK." Being divorced was not OK with me. I never spoke the words once.

Still, God's love and purpose in my life could not be ignored. Bobbie's words of wisdom, God's clear favor in my life, and His giving me the desires of my heart made it hard to ignore His lovingkindness. Sometimes it became clear through the open pages of my Bible, sometimes in the tender words spoken by a fellow sojourner, and sometimes in the still small voice inside me. The messages always pointed toward God's love. All I had to do was live in it.

God continued to provide for me and my children. He wrote me a new story. See, He's always moving to draw us closer. That's His definition of success: being close to His children. Being successful in His eyes is simply being able to accept the love He paid such a high price to give us. I'm thankful that it's always His plan to lavish us with that love.

> Psalm 136:1 (NIV)
>
> Give thanks to the Lord, for he is good. His love endures forever.

JONI TOPPER, also known as the GloryTeller, radiates the glory of God, sharing everyday moments in compelling storyteller fashion. This Granna, author, worship leader, speaker, and cofounder of Uprooted Women, a spirit-filled one-day women's event, is passionate about "being" the church. Joni emanates joy. She and her pastor husband, Ernest, have served in the same church for thirty years.

Joni's award-winning debut book, *The Power of a Well-Placed Yes: God's Abundant Faithfulness in a Small Church,* launched in March 2024. She's contributed to six other collaborations.

Joni is excited to meet you!

Connect with Joni on her website at jonitopper.com.

CHAPTER 18

Seasons of Redefined Motherhood

IT IS A PARADOX my heart still struggles to explain. I have never heard a child call me Mom, but I have little voices that squeal "Graham!" with unrestrained joy.

Winter: The Season of Longing

Winter on the farm is a time of waiting. The fields lie dormant under blankets of snow, seeds buried deep, holding potential not yet visible. For much of my life, my heart resembled those winter fields, harboring dreams of motherhood beneath the surface.

For as long as I can remember, I wanted to be a mom, not in a casual, "maybe someday" way, but with the confident tug of a calling. As a little girl, I imagined bedtime stories, first-day-of-school pictures, sticky toddler kisses, and family dinners around the table. Motherhood wasn't just a hope; it felt like part of who God made me to be.

After a painful divorce in my early thirties, my dream of raising children felt increasingly out of reach. When I met Farmer, a steady, kindhearted man who loved both the land and the Lord, hope stirred again. He had four children from his previous marriage. By then, I was in my late thirties, and I wondered if God might be answering my prayer in a different way.

However, being a stepmom is not the same as being a biological mom. Farmer's children were twenty-one, nineteen, sixteen, and ten when we married. The empty place in my heart for "my" children remained. And though I tried to be grateful, there was still that small voice whispering, "This isn't the same."

Spring: The Season of Hope and Loss

Three years into our marriage, it happened: I was pregnant. Just as spring brings the first green shoots pushing through thawing ground, new life was growing in me. I can still remember the joy that day. Each wave of nausea whispered, "This is real." I prayed over that little life every day and pictured the moment I would finally hold him or her in my arms.

Spring on the farm is a season of vulnerability. Tender shoots can be damaged by a late frost; new life requires protection. And then came the day that changed everything.

At nearly twelve weeks, we went in for an ultrasound, eager for our first glimpse. Instead of a steady heartbeat, the room filled with silence. The technician's face told me before her words did: there was no life.

Then came the second shock. "There are two babies," she said. Twins. I hadn't known there were two. In a single breath, I learned both the magnitude of what I'd been given and the reality that I had lost them both. My dreams doubled and shattered all at once.

The timing cut deep. Just three weeks later, we celebrated the wedding of our oldest son. I smiled for pictures, hugged guests, and did my best to rejoice with our family. Inside, I was shattered.

The months that followed were heavy with grief. I clung to hope in quiet moments, praying for another child, but over time, God's answer became clear: no.

That "no" was hard. I wrestled with it, asking the questions that surface when our deepest desires go unfulfilled: *Why, Lord? Why allow this longing only to have it unmet? Why give me the twins and then take them before I can even hold them?*

Yet even in my pain, He whispered comfort: "Before I formed you in the womb I knew you" (Jeremiah 1:5 NIV). In the quiet, He reminded me I was a mother. My babies were real. They were known. He gave me a tender picture of Him holding my daughter, and my mom holding my son. The ache didn't vanish, but the sharp edges softened.

Another verse anchored me in that season. "The Lord is close to the brokenhearted and saves those who are crushed in spirit" (Psalm 34:18 NIV). My spirit was certainly crushed, but He kept showing up, sometimes through His Word, sometimes through a friend's hug, sometimes through the silent comfort of knowing He saw every tear.

Summer: The Season of Unexpected Abundance

Then, fourteen months after my twins should have been born, my first grandchild arrived. Like summer's sudden abundance after spring's uncertainty, this blessing caught me by surprise.

Becoming a grandmother had never been on my radar. I had never felt like "Mom," so grandchildren weren't part of my dreams. I asked God to help me love them for who they were, not for what I didn't have. He answered.

Today, I am Graham to eight grandchildren: two bright and talented eleven-year-old boys; a cartwheeling, fun-loving nine-year-old girl; a jokester eight-year-old boy; a curious, rough-and-tumble six-year-old boy; a spunky five-year-old girl; a thoughtful, tenderhearted four-year-old girl; and a smiley, carbon-copy-of-Farmer nine-month-old boy.

Summer on the farm brings an abundance of life, fields heavy with grain, gardens overflowing, days stretched long with light and activity. My Mondays with four of the grandchildren mirror this vibrancy. It's my favorite kind of beautiful chaos—school pickups and snack negotiations, blocks toppling and belly laughs, sand-filled shoes, and "Watch me, Graham!" ricocheting through the farmyard.

The nine-year-old is doing backflips across the lawn. The six-year-old barrels toward the shop to see what Grandpa is doing. The tender four-year-old, who loves catching toads and splashing in puddles, climbs into my lap with muddy hands and pats my cheek. "You okay, Graham?" My Wednesdays with the baby—oh, that grin—he looks up at me with Farmer's eyes and an entire morning's worth of joy.

Summer days are full of motion-tractor rides along fence lines, the rumble of four-wheelers across pastures with small bodies pressed against mine, bowling balls thundering down lanes followed by victory dances. Sometimes, in the middle of this summer abundance, I pause. *This was never the path I pictured,* I tell the Lord. *But look at what You have given me. Thank you!*

Autumn: The Season of Harvest and Reflection

I never had grandparents of my own; all of mine were gone before I was born. Maybe that's why being Graham feels so sacred. I get to offer what I never knew firsthand: a steady presence, a listening ear, a soft place to land. I'm not the disciplinarian or the daily decision-maker. I'm the one who delights, shows up, and prays over scraped knees, math tests, and tender hearts.

Autumn on the farm is harvest time, when the work of previous seasons yields its fruit. In this autumn season of my life, I'm gathering memories instead of children, collecting moments that nourish my soul.

Healing didn't arrive in a single, triumphant moment. It came like autumn light—golden, gentle, illuminating, ordinary beauty. It came through Monday card games at the kitchen table, serious concentration on small faces, giggles between rounds. It came in the smell of brownies baking, Legos clicking into place, whispered prayers at naptime, and the *voom voom* of the tractor while the baby naps on my chest.

It came through a thousand small yeses: yes to one more story, yes to puddle-jumping in rain boots, yes to celebrating their wins, yes to loving without claiming. Grief and joy learned to share a house, like the bitter-sweet beauty of autumn, where leaves change color even as they prepare to fall.

My story has never looked like the one I dreamed of as a girl. No one calls me Mom. Yet I am living a calling all the same. Psalm 113:9 (HCSB) says, "He gives the childless woman a household, making her the joyful mother of children. Hallelujah!" God did not answer my prayers in the way I envisioned, but He answered them in a way that has filled my lap and my life.

Success in God's eyes was never about titles, timelines, or ticking the boxes I once held so tightly. It has looked like faithful surrender, trusting Him when the answer was no. It has looked like stewardship, loving the family He placed in my life, not the one I imagined. It has looked like a purpose, pointing little hearts toward Him.

I didn't get the story I thought I wanted. I got the story He wrote for me. And it is good.

So here I am, a mother whose arms are still waiting for two precious children in heaven, and a Graham whose lap and heart are full on earth.

This is my motherhood—success in His eyes, harvested across all seasons.

> Galatians 6:9 (NIV)
> Let us not become weary in doing good, for at the proper time we will reap a harvest if we do not give up.

RAYNA NEISES is an author, speaker, and certified coach who helps women find hope in the hard seasons of caregiving, waiting, and loss. She is the author of *No Regrets: Hope for Your Caregiving Season* and host of the *A Season of Caring Podcast*.

Rayna knows firsthand the ache of infertility and miscarriage, as well as the long journey of caring for both parents with Alzheimer's. Her story is woven with pain, but also with God's tender mercies and surprising gifts—like becoming "Graham" to her grandchildren even when she least expected it.

In addition to her speaking and coaching, Rayna also offers virtual assistant and web design services, helping leaders and organizations manage their work with ease so they can focus on what matters most.

Rayna lives on a farm in Kansas, where wide-open skies remind her daily of God's faithfulness. She is passionate about helping women discover joy, strength, and peace—even in life's hardest seasons.

Connect with Rayna on her website at RaynaNeises.com.

Chapter 19

Not Medicine, but Healing

Some people measure success by education, career, and income. Others see it in a happy marriage and a life devoted to raising children. I wanted it all. I longed to be present for my children's early years while still answering what I thought was a call to the medical field. My plan was perfect: I would stay home until my youngest child started school, then pursue nursing.

But life rarely goes according to plan.

On December 5, 2006, my precious five-year-old son, Mason, died suddenly and unexpectedly after a medical mistake deprived him of oxygen and left him brain-dead. My life before that time had already been peppered with grief experiences, including the deaths of my father, my older stepbrother, and my sister. But nothing could have prepared me for the loss of my own child.

Just two weeks earlier, Mason and I went shopping for a Christmas tree. I normally wait until after Thanksgiving to set up the tree, but a major cold front was on the way, and I thought it would be the perfect time. The day began beautifully with sunny skies and temperatures in the high sixties. We bounced into the garden section full of excitement, enjoying our time together. I told Mason all about the snuggle weather that was headed our way, and we shrieked with excitement when we felt the first surge of icy air hit our skin. By the time we got home, the temperature had plummeted almost forty degrees. Our beautiful day was now painfully bitter as we unloaded the car. I had no idea that my beautiful life was about to change just as suddenly and bitterly. One day, we were preparing for Christmas, and the next, we were preparing to bury our child.

It has often been said that raising a child should come with an instruction book. For me, raising my children came naturally. I loved everything about being a mother.

I was blessed with a supportive husband who valued that calling and supported me being home with our children, as well as an amazing support system in my sister and sister-in-law. I loved them both and held a deep admiration for how they mothered their own children. They became my blueprints, my living guidebooks, my torchbearers. Whatever they did is what I would do, and from the moment my tiny firstborn daughter was placed in my arms, I felt completely prepared for motherhood.

What I was not prepared for, and what even they could not prepare me for, was the death of my child. I remember thinking that if the pain I felt continued, I would die. There was no relief, no escape. Worse still was knowing my older children were hurting just as deeply, and I was powerless to ease their pain. I knew I would have to be intentional if I was going to survive this loss.

My sister and sister-in-law had once been my blueprints in motherhood. In the valley of death, I longed for that same kind of example—those whose survival could prove that mine was possible, whose endurance could carry a light into my darkness and remind me that God still makes survival possible, even in the aftermath of child loss.

As much as I admired the women in my life, I knew I needed a connection with other bereaved parents. God is faithful to provide our every need, and even before Mason's funeral, people from within my own church began to share their own experiences of child loss with me. Some were recent, some had taken place decades earlier. Their stories had one thread in common: a desire to encourage me and my husband, to let us know we could survive the devastation of child loss. I also noticed something else. Those who truly encouraged me never did so without pointing me to God's Word.

In the months that followed, I realized that my "instruction book" for how to survive the death of a child was the Bible. It contained everything I needed to know about surviving grief. When I felt sorry for myself, God pointed me to Matthew 5:45 and reminded me that I didn't deserve the joys of this life any more than I deserved the sorrows. When I felt sad, He gave me Psalm 30:5 (NKJV): "Weeping may endure for a night, but joy comes in the morning." When I questioned why I had to suffer, He gave me 2 Corinthians 1:3–4. God's Word continually met me in my sorrow. Still, even with Scripture as my anchor, I knew I couldn't walk this road alone. I needed living examples of faith from parents who had survived child loss to walk beside me.

I came to realize that every parent who loses a beloved child will experience grief. We have little choice in that, but grieving well and choosing to live with purpose is within our power.

To live out grief with faith is not the same as being strong. In fact, 2 Corinthians 12:9 tells us His grace is sufficient, and His power is made perfect in weakness. Weakness leads to surrender. And it is in surrender, not in understanding, that we find peace.

The week Mason died, I was desperately seeking the Lord. My prayers were cries for survival: How will I make it through this? How will I help my children heal when my own heart feels destroyed? I knew I had to survive the funeral for my husband and my children, but that's as far as my mind could carry me into the future. I could not wrap my mind around living the next five, ten, or twenty years carrying the weight of the pain I felt.

I don't like putting words in God's mouth, but in the midst of that wrestling, I felt a deep stirring in my heart, as if He was impressing upon me a promise: "I will give you a servant's heart, and in serving, you will find healing." I almost laughed through my tears. A servant's heart? That was the last thing I saw in myself. I couldn't fathom serving others when I was barely surviving. I tucked those words away, thinking I must have imagined them. It would be years before I began to understand the significance of that promise.

We are so blessed that the hospital where Mason spent his last week offered the services of Child Life Specialists. Before Mason was taken off life support, they helped my older children create keepsake handprints that became one of my most cherished treasures. I didn't know then how important those handprints would be.

A few months after Mason's passing, a high school friend of mine lost her baby to SIDS. My heart broke for her. I knew too well the pain of walking out of the hospital with empty arms. As I sat with her loss, I thought about Mason's handprints. They brought me a tangible comfort I could not put into words. And then I wondered if I could create that same tangible comfort for her. That thought became a seed.

In giving to others what had brought me comfort, I stepped into the healing I felt God had promised.

I didn't realize it at the time, but that was my call to action regarding the servant's heart. Out of my brokenness, something unexpected began to grow. What began as a single act of compassion became a ministry. Over the years, it has grown to reach hundreds of families. Looking back now, I see the thread I couldn't see then. I see how God took my shattered heart and reshaped it into something that could pour out comfort for others. I see how He fulfilled the promise I felt He had whispered to me in the darkest week of my life—that He would give me a servant's heart, and in serving, I would find healing.

Our first Christmas without Mason came just weeks after his death. The holidays were unbearable for many years. Each Thanksgiving, the dread set in, and I just tried to focus on making it through December. I tried my best to give my older children joyous memories, but I always felt like a failure. In time, I realized how common this cycle is for grieving families, and I felt a special pull to reach out to grieving parents specifically during the holidays. Out of that pain came our Christmas Ornament Outreach.

We create personalized Christmas ornaments that offer grieving families a small but tangible comfort during the holidays. Our Christmas cards, designed with grieving parents in mind, bring added encouragement to those who are hurting. Each year, my church and others commit to praying throughout the holidays for the families who receive this outreach. It is a simple yet powerful way to bring comfort to grieving hearts.

For our family, the Christmas Ornament Outreach became part of our healing. I will always treasure the memories of us gathered around the bar, shaping clay and creating ornaments together. What might have been a season only marked by pain began to hold moments of connection, laughter, and purpose. Those times reminded us that healing can be found not just in receiving comfort but in giving it away.

Over time, what began with prints and ornaments grew into more. We began hosting retreats for grieving parents and sewing tiny burial gowns for families saying goodbye to stillborn or premature babies. Each new layer of the ministry felt like another way God was redeeming Mason's story.

As I was training a volunteer to create the prints, her pastor's wife asked to observe. When we were finished and stepped outside the funeral home, she began to weep. I apologized and told her I should have better prepared her for the experience of seeing a lifeless child. I will never forget her explaining that she wasn't crying because of that. She was crying because she felt like she had been standing on holy ground. To this day, I've found no better words to describe this experience.

My passion for nursing never returned. The trauma of losing my son and spending that week in the hospital left me unable to imagine functioning in a medical setting again. But God, in His mercy, gave me a new direction. I once believed my calling was to care for the sick through medicine. Instead, He gave me the privilege of comforting the brokenhearted, to offer tangible comfort in their darkest moments, and to bring hope where words so often fail.

When I asked God how I would survive five, ten, or twenty years into the future, I think I expected to be healed by this point. I never imagined that, almost twenty years later, I would just now be where I'm supposed to be. There have been many setbacks along the way, and I've had to step back at times, but the healing is still unfolding.

Everything I do flows out of Mason's life and the loss that forever changed mine. I learned that I could not walk that path until I surrendered my pain into God's hands. But that is not just my story; it is a truth for every heart walking through sorrow. We may not have a choice in whether grief or trials come, but we do have a choice in how we respond. And when we surrender our pain to Him, it doesn't mean the road becomes pain-free. But it does mean His peace will meet us there. I have no doubt the work I do brings comfort to broken hearts, and I know I have followed the path God set before me. In God's eyes and mine, that is success. Looking back, I see that He did not take away my calling, He transformed it. Not medicine, but healing.

Galatians 6:2 (NIV)
Carry each other's burdens, and in this way
you will fulfill the law of Christ.

DAISY THIEBAUD, while not a grief expert, carries lived experience with profound loss and ministers to others who have also experienced this kind of loss. She shares her story not because it is special, but because she knows newly bereaved parents need to hear the stories of others, just as she once did.

Her ministry, Hopeprints Ministries, was created as a work of comfort and compassion for grieving families. She partners with churches and focuses on retreats that help communities become places where sorrow is met with compassion and hope—because no one should walk through grief alone.

Daisy lives in Southeast Texas and is a wife, a mother, and the proud "Shugie" to her cystic fibrosis warrior, Fletcher, the truest calling she has ever stepped into.

Connect with Daisy on her website at Hopeprints.org.

CHAPTER 20

Finding Hope in Waiting

WAITING. JUST SEEING THAT word can create all kinds of reactions. We wait at the doctor's office, the dentist's office, and the grocery store line. None of it is fun. It is just part of life. Waiting means we really don't have control. We are at the mercy of the place or situation currently happening.

There is a different kind of waiting—when God is in control of the timing. He uses this waiting to teach us about Him. We learn that He isn't in a hurry. He controls it all. If we are willing, we can develop a deep, abiding, and trusting relationship with this wonderful Savior Who wants to teach us so much more than just receiving what we desire.

Abraham waited for his promised son. He and his wife, Sarah, were impatient, took matters into their own hands, and caused an uproar in their home. When it was God's time, Isaac was born, God's gift to them.

Joseph had prophetic dreams, but not enough spiritual maturity to carry the weight of them. He went through much preparation before God could allow him to carry the leadership that He called him to fulfill.

Through great sorrow, I began at a young age, in my late twenties, learning the importance of waiting on God. We started our family and had two wonderful sons born to us. Yet, some years later, I desired a little girl. I became pregnant and miscarried at ten weeks. Two more times, I became pregnant and miscarried both babies. At this point, I was physically weary, and my body needed rest. We waited a while, and I became pregnant again. Within a few months, we found out I was pregnant with twins. There was great excitement, yet some complications developed six months into the pregnancy, and I went into labor early. I gave birth to beautiful, identical twin boys, but they were very tiny and only lived for two days.

After returning home, I lay by my bed sobbing and talking to Jesus, asking for strength, not understanding why all this was happening to me. He spoke very clearly and lovingly to my heart.

I'm going to give you your Amy, the desire of your heart, but it must be in my time. I knew then God would fulfill His promise. I also began that day, at the age of twenty-eight, to seriously learn the lesson of waiting upon God for strength and His timing. It would be one of the most significant spiritual lessons I would ever learn. Waiting on God for His timing and strength brings peace and clarity in all of life's decisions. Several years later, our Amy Joy was born, just as the Lord promised, in His time.

God does His best work in the waiting room. You may have prayed for a job situation, issues with a spouse, or not having a spouse. You may have a financial need, a health issue, or a heart wound that few are aware of. Maybe you feel alone and helpless, or maybe you feel great and on top of the world, and yet, there's something missing.

The waiting room is a place where God longs to be with you and me. It's a time when we learn to depend on Him because He alone has the answer. The waiting draws us to the only One Who can meet the need. He is sovereign. He is Lord. In that holy role, He wants to teach us that He can be trusted to meet our needs. He wants us to come to Him and not try to do it on our own. There is so much to learn in the waiting room. Let's look at some of the ways God moves.

It takes a while to learn the power that comes through prayer. Prayer is a place of surrender. We realize our God is the One Who answers. We take things to Him and learn that He answers in His way and His timing. His answer is not always what we desire. Sometimes His answer is no or not now, and it can be never. We learn we can trust He knows what He is doing. The Scriptures state: "Wait for the Lord; be strong and take heart and wait for the Lord" (Psalms 27:14 NIV).

When we pray, we can surrender the need to have our way. We allow Him to be Lord, and peace comes. If we are striving and pushing for our way, our timing, our answer, peace doesn't come. But when we truly surrender, at times with many tears, peace will come.

Prayer is also the place where we find clarity in situations. We need guidance in our relationships. Jesus can give wisdom in how to deal with things that overwhelm us. This is one of the reasons I've learned over the years to make it a priority in my life to have prayer time first thing in my morning. I know this is not always possible if you have small children.

When my husband was in the Navy, we had two small boys. He was overseas, so I had no privacy time. I had to wait until naptime to have uninterrupted prayer times. Jesus knows what we need. He knows the challenges that will come in the day. He gives supernatural strength and wisdom to deal with the situations because we commit the day to Him and His leading.

He is also an always available God. Think about the many times in the day when you say, "Lord, help," because He has the answer. You have learned He is a loving God Who wants to meet your needs and answer your prayers. He is the ultimate Father Who loves you with everlasting love and answers with what is best for you. So, prayer is our place of surrender to a loving God Who knows best.

When we learn to let go, wonderful rest comes to our souls. One of the most powerful places we can be in is at rest. We aren't working at it anymore. We let go of control, so hard for us to do, and find God really sees us and wants to be close to us. We can be led by His Spirit and find our choices are more effective, powerful, and helpful to others.

When our peace is disturbed, something is not right. It's a great indicator that we may be taking the wrong direction. This is why waiting upon God in prayer is such a powerful way to find clarity. Long before I was in ministry, I worked in medicine. There were times over the years when I was applying for various jobs. I asked Jesus to show me which one was right and close the doors on the others. I also followed the peace in my spirit. We recently prayed at the altar at our church with a lady new to our church and our area who was looking for a job. We encouraged her to follow peace and prayed that the Lord would make it clear. She's had multiple opportunities, but just didn't feel right about them. God brings great rest to those who follow His leading.

Matthew 11:28–30 (NIV) states it very clearly. "Come to me, all you who are weary and burdened, and I will give you rest. Take my yoke upon you and learn from me, for I am gentle and humble in heart, and you will find rest for your souls. For my yoke is easy and my burden is light." We can become very weary when we try to carry our own load. Just take it to Jesus. He alone can carry you and bring you through.

There are times in our lives when God will give us a specific promise. Sometimes, He will place a specific desire in our hearts. We try to fulfill that desire and find out we can't make it happen. God has His own timetable in His leading of our lives. Because of His love for us, He knows what is best.

As you walk through your life journey, you may have many opportunities to wait for a desire to be answered. You may have heavy challenges in your life today. One of the most loving things God can do is teach us to wait for His timing. Most of the time, it doesn't make sense to us. After all, these desires seem perfectly legitimate. Yet, because He loves us so much, He calls us to wait and trust Him. If you have been a parent, you know not everything is best for your children. Because we love them so much, we don't always give them everything they want. In the same way, God loves us so much and knows what is best for us. He delights in blessing us, but He knows the best time for blessing us.

I want to end this time with a favorite Scripture of mine. I encourage you to insert your name in place of the words you, they, and those; read it aloud. Jesus is more than enough to give you all you need. As you wait for Him by praying, resting, and trusting His timing in your life, He will show His love and mercy in all your needs.

Isaiah 40:28–31 (NASB)

Do you not know? Have you not heard? The Everlasting God, the Lord, the Creator of the ends of the earth does not become weary or tired. His understanding is unsearchable. He gives strength to the weary, and to the one who lacks might He increases power. Though youths grow weary and tired, and vigorous young men stumble badly, yet those who wait for the Lord will gain new strength; They will mount up with wings like eagles, they will run and not get tired; they will walk and not become weary.

SHAREN LONG, author of *Heart's Desire* and contributing author to *Still Speaking,* brings joy as a singer, speaker, and minister who radiates warmth and encouragement wherever she goes. Having personally experienced the deep sorrow of losing babies, Sharen now comforts others walking that same difficult path through both her writing and speaking ministry. She loves teaching women about God's faithfulness and stands ready to pray with them for their needs, believing in the special closeness that forms when two women agree together in prayer. Through her story, she offers hope, healing, and the gentle reminder that when we place our pain in Jesus' hands, we are never alone. Sharen loves the color red and possesses a unique gift for giving animals their own distinctive voices, much to the pet owner's delight.

Connect with Sharen on her website at sharenlong.com.

CHAPTER 21

Unstoppable Success!

THEY SAY THAT WOMEN have an instinct to love, nurture, and protect their children. But what happens when a mother is damaged before she bears that title? Indeed, this is a heavy subject to broach, but is there any lasting healing, deliverance, or change for the better if deep-rooted issues are not addressed?

I say, no. Experience has taught me that secrets and silent frustration only make things worse over time. Time can heal old wounds if those wounds are dealt with, detoxified, bandaged, and given the proper time and patience for nature's scar to signify the completion of the healing process. This is true for the soul as well, spiritually speaking.

Moms are celebrated on a yearly basis for their giving, their patience, their overextending, their denial of self and self-care—in lieu of the benevolence they bestow on others. Most will only celebrate moms by what they see with their eyes or feel with their hearts. Outward shows of sentiment—flowers, perfume, jewelry, crayon drawings, noodle art, and freshly picked weeds snatched from the ground with momma's smiling face in mind, all mean to say, "Thank you, Mother, you're the best."

But what about the mom who struggled to get up out of her bed of depression to dutifully prepare breakfast, even if it was just instant oatmeal or cold cereal?

What do we think of the mom who fearfully sheltered her babies so suffocatingly that they left home early to declare their autonomy, thus further causing the mother to suffer prolonged, undue stress?

What about the mom teetering on the edge of sanity who ignores knocks at her door, who hides for days behind closed window blinds? Or the mom who sustains a false sense of worth by living vicariously through celebrities she watches on TV. She's counted herself out of life, accepting impoverishment of spirit as her portion. This mom lives a meager existence versus flourishing in her purpose, tormented by the gifts and talents that won't let her accept inertia. She deals with restlessness that is accompanied by fear because she perceives that this is not what her life was meant to be.

What about the mom who chose to have children because *he* wanted them and *he* believed that she had enough love in her and that he had enough love in him to draw hers out of her sheltered heart?

How about the mom who feared she'd infect her children with her mental instability and emotional ineptness—fearing life's evils—so she hid them under her skirt tail, determined to protect them from the cruel, harsh world that infected her mind and soul? Do these moms deserve recognition, accolades, and respect? I say, yes.

How about the teen mom who never planned to be a mom so soon, but for her, abortion wasn't an option. Or how about the woman who was forced, or chose, to abort her child out of demand, obligation, fear, shame, anger, indignation, or inconvenience. How about she who is plagued with her baby's phantom cries in the silence of her midnight hours?

What about the single mom who naively assumed that, if she became pregnant, her boyfriend would marry her. Or the married mom who thought, "Surely he won't leave me if I give him the child he wants."

If you are her, I am she, sent to encourage you that you, too, are successful in God's eyes. You see, your actions and past mistakes don't define your status with your heavenly Father. It was Jesus' passion that paved the way for your righteousness with the Father. You are *not* "a sinner saved by grace," you are simply "saved"—by the grace and mercy of Jesus Christ. He will not return to the cross for you; it was a one-and-done, once-for-all assignment that is *finished*. No longer are you an unrighteous sinner without right-standing with the Father, but you are a child of God, born so by your confession of Jesus Christ:

"But to all who believed him and accepted him, he gave the *right* to become children of God. They are reborn—not with a physical birth resulting from human passion or plan, but a birth that comes from God" (John 1:12–13 NLT, emphasis mine).

If you have accepted Jesus Christ as your Lord and Savior, you are already a success in God's eyes. By your wise decision, made with your free will, your status is no longer "sinner," but "saint." To declare yourself a sinner is to say that Jesus didn't get the job done for you. Nothing could be further from the truth:

"And so, God willing, we will move forward to further understanding. For it is impossible to bring back to repentance those who were once enlightened—those who have experienced the good things of heaven and shared in the Holy Spirit, who have tasted the goodness of the word of God and the power of the age to come—and who then turn away from God. It is impossible to bring such people back to repentance; by rejecting the Son of God, they themselves are nailing him to the cross once again and holding him up to public shame" (Hebrews 6:3–6 NLT).

You are not her, mentioned above, therefore you must speak life over yourself, no matter what your circumstances are. The truth is that you were once a sinner, but now you are the righteous and anointed daughter of God. If your daughter said to you, "I'm so ugly," or "I'm such a stupid failure," wouldn't you reprove and affirm her in the *truth*? How much more would the Holy Spirit's compassion speak to your negative, life-depleting words spoken over yourself? In truth, it is a form of false humility to declare yourself a sinner when you've been born again.

God *always* wants you to speak life—only—over yourself and your loved ones.

Are we now clear about those who *are* sinners, who are "rejecting the Son of God" and "nailing him to the cross once again . . . holding him up to public shame?" Rather, you are blessed to have been "accepted in the Beloved," and Jesus has given you eternal life (Ephesians 1:6 NKJV). He says, "Neither shall anyone snatch [you] out of My hand" (John 10:28 NKJV).

You may be thinking, "Why is she so enthusiastic about making this point?" Allow me to explain. In order to halt your feelings of not being successful in God's eyes—of feeling like a failure, a sinner, or one with imposter syndrome—you must first *know* that your works, giving, selflessness, others' opinions, tormenting thoughts, and anything else has nothing to do with you being a success in God's eyes.

First, understand, mother, that God loves you with a fervent love. His love for you has nothing to do with your performance or nonperformance. There is nothing you can do to make God love you more, and there is nothing you can do to make God love you less. He just loves you; in fact, He adores you!

As a mother whose children left home in their mid-teens—Yes, I am much of "her" spoken of in the introduction of this story—God has made me fully aware that I am not the only woman who has been tormented by feelings of failure as a mother. It was He who chose this topic for my contribution to this anthology. Honestly, I would have preferred that this cup would have passed me by. Nonetheless, I made a vow a long time ago to follow the Holy Spirit's guidance to effect healing and deliverance in the lives of those wounded in spirit.

Therefore, allow me to address the mother who has endured an abortion. I was date-raped as a teenager, and it led to my becoming pregnant. Much of my circumstances was due to my low self-value, not realizing my significance in Christ, and not having a support system as a teen runaway.

Before that, I was sexually abused as a minor by the pastor of my cult-church. I ran away and have fended for myself ever since. Old habits die hard, but they do die. As a result of my becoming a pregnant teenager, my permissive father took me "home" to my authoritarian mother, but I did not stay.

After a family meeting ensued between my boyfriend's parents and mine, it was decided that I would have an abortion against my will. Financial arrangements were made between the adults and the appointment to terminate my pregnancy was set. My mother, disappointed, embarrassed, and incensed, threw me to the floor when no one was present, save my fifteen-year-old boyfriend, kicked me in my belly, and proclaimed that I was "getting 'it' out of me." That did not result in a spontaneous abortion; therefore, I was forced to endure an induced abortion at a clinic in a nearby city.

I've shared this to say that it wasn't until seventeen years after I ran from the cult-church where children were sexually abused and it was covered up by the adulterous and duplicitous flock of believers there, that I had a powerful God-encounter that began my journey of healing and the reestablishing of my Christ-esteem. You can read the full story in my book, *Making Heaven My Home*.

I mustered the courage to return to the God Whom I'd once trusted and loved, and He restored my soul. About my aborted baby, He told me, "That which was lost will be found again." From that intimation, I later received, in prayer, that no one has more power than the Giver of life. No parent, no person, no criminal, no abortionist—*no one*. The wisdom of God is indescribably amazing!

I want to encourage you that we are spirits who live in bodies, and we have souls. Babies are spirits as well, intended to fulfill a specific purpose just like us. The termination of breath in the body caused by the cessation of the heartbeat does not kill the *spirit*. Granted, it ends the continued process of life as we know it, but there is no human will greater than the will, power, and authority of our Mighty God. In sum, call me crazy, but I believe that nothing we do to take a life can kill the spirit where life eternal truly is.

For example, we will have glorified bodies, we born-again believers, when we've been raptured at Christ's second coming, but we don't know what we'll look like. Scripture only informs us that we will be like Christ as He now appears in His glory:

Dear friends, we are already God's children, but he has not yet shown us what we will be like when Christ appears. But we do know that we will be like him, for we will see him as he really is. (1 John 3:2 NLT)

And guess what, mother? We'll be reunited with the spirit-souls of our departed loved ones, despite the means of their departure. "All souls are mine," says God, both the parents and the children alike (Ezekiel 18:4 ESV). That includes innocent babies. Be encouraged, God is magnificent and His ways ineffable. You may not be able to wrap your brain around it, but please receive in your spirit that "that which was lost" to you will also "be found again," beloved mother. And by your confession, you are forgiven.

Jesus was murdered at His crucifixion by the order of a kangaroo court. Nevertheless, He is no more dead than the sleeping believer or the innocent baby.

Regarding the mother whose children have willfully ghosted her, let me encourage you as well. I have four biological, adult children who infrequently contact me. There are many layers of dysfunction and reasons that may or may not be like yours. Know that your prayers and fasting will make more of an impact in your children's lives than anything else you can do. Your "earnest prayer" as a righteous mother "has great power and produces wonderful results" (James 5:16 NLT). You must believe that the Creator of all life is fully capable and desirous to restore *everything* that this life has stripped from you, whether by your sins or those committed against you. "But if we confess our sins to him, he is faithful and just to forgive us our sins and to cleanse us from all wickedness" (1 John 1:9 NLT).

It was by your confession as a sinner, mother, that you received Jesus Christ as your Lord and Savior. And it is by the confession of your sins, as a *child of God* (not a sinner), that you are forgiven and cleansed from the depravity of your flesh.

In conclusion, rejoice, mother! You are a success in God's eyes because God's definition of success is simply, "being who you were created to be while doing what you were created to do."[1] Leave the past behind, along with those who ostracize, judge, abuse, and promote lies that lead you to think you're a failure. Your destiny will not be determined by what people say about you. Discover your divine purpose and be a success on your way to destiny. Nothing can stop you because the anointing (God's presence, love, and power with you) makes you unstoppable.

Joshua 1:9 (BSB)
Have I not commanded you to be strong and courageous?
Do not be afraid; do not be discouraged,
for the Lord your God is with you wherever you go.

MARY-JEANETTE SMITH is a speaker and transformational coach who equips women to heal from emotional and spiritual wounds to LYLA!™ (Live Your Life Affirmed!). Her compelling story of overcoming church hurt, sexual abuse, intimate partner violence, and divorce guides women to soar in their identity in Christ.

Mary-Jeanette has administered healing for thirty-two years in churches, support groups, and residentials. She has spoken on multiple platforms, including nationally at PTWWN TV.

She is the award-winning author of *Making Heaven My Home* and the recently released *Living Affirmed: How to Walk Confidently in Your Divine Purpose.*

She is a foodie, home chef, and theater buff who delights in all things weddings.

Connect with Mary-Jeanette on her website at
mjeanettesmith.com/connect-with-m-j/

---

1. M.J. Smith, *Living Affirmed: How to Walk Confidently in Your Divine Purpose,* (Trilogy Christian Publishing, 2025).

CHAPTER 22

The Mirror Lied to Me

For as long as I can remember, I carried a quiet tension inside, the feeling that I needed to be less of myself to be more accepted. It wasn't always loud. In fact, it often whispered in subtle comments, unspoken expectations, and cultural ideals that quietly made their way into my heart and mind. Somewhere along the way, I began to believe that if I could just be smaller, thinner, quieter, and more "together," then maybe I would finally be enough. I can vaguely recall the pain and shame that it caused.

At the age of thirty-three, after completing a medically supervised weight loss program, something shifted inside me. What started as a pursuit of health spiraled into a full-blown eating disorder. It did not happen overnight. Initially, I simply started restricting my diet. Then came the episodes of bingeing, eating all the food I loved. Then purging. I'd make myself throw up all the food I ate and cry afterwards.

At times, my body responded without being prompted. I did not even have to force myself to purge. It just happened, and that is what really frightened me.

When it came to my eating habits, it was either nothing at all or everything I could find. I was caught in a cycle of extremes with food. I was losing control in the name of trying to have control. Just imagine—I was an oncology doctor who was familiar with medical issues, yet I was powerless to help myself with my own.

My mindset was all over the place, it seemed. Yet all of it hidden, all of it heavy. But the weight I carried wasn't just physical. It was mental, emotional, and spiritual.

Mentally, I couldn't see myself as I actually was. My mind skewed my reality. Body dysmorphia twisted what I saw in the mirror as the person staring back at me bore no resemblance to who I truly was. The reflection was distorted, not by the glass, but by years of internalized lies: pressure, perfectionism, and shame.

At first, I did not want to talk about it. Disordered eating can feel like a silent addiction, one that masquerades as discipline, control, or even wellness. Emotionally, it was breaking me from the inside out. However, a single moment in time changed everything. My Christian counselor, a kind and deeply grounded believer, looked me in the eye and said something that cracked the darkness wide open:

"You've been loved all along. You just didn't know it."

It wasn't just a good word. It was the truth. And the truth started to set me free.

Pairing therapy with Scripture became a lifeline for me. It marked the beginning of my healing process in every way. Isn't it interesting that when we start healing spiritually, we also find physical, mental, and emotional healing?

I grew up reading the Bible, and I am grateful that my mother insisted on it. Isaiah 43 became my anchor. Those verses began to rewrite the narrative that had ruled my inner life for so long:

"Fear not, for I am with you ... When you pass through the waters, I will be with you ... You are mine. You are precious and honored in my sight" (Isaiah 43:1–2, 4–5, my paraphrase).

For the first time, I began to believe I was more than a number on a scale or the size of my clothes. I was created for God's glory. I was already accepted. Already enough. I am grateful for the power of the Word of God that sustains me daily.

People often ask, "Are you fully recovered now?"

My answer? Recovery is daily. Just like someone in recovery from addiction, I walk it out every single day, with God's grace and with intention. Psalm 46:1 (NIV) says, "God is our refuge and strength, an ever-present help in trouble." My help truly comes from the Lord. He is my strength. Without him, I could not face this disorder. But with him, I face it and conquer it day by day.

What helps me the most is starting the day with the Lord. Early in the morning, before the world's noise drowns out the voice of God, I sit with my Bible, read Scripture, journal, and simply listen. Those quiet moments are where I draw strength, not just to resist old patterns, but to walk in freedom.

I have come to understand that it is not *just* about what I eat physically. It is about what I feed myself spiritually and emotionally. I have learned that peace does not come from control; it comes from surrender to God.

Surrender doesn't come easily to everyone. But I was determined to give what I could to the Lord every day. I was desperate for the freedom that

I recognized came with more surrender. So, I give all I can to the Lord, and He sustains me.

If you are reading this and wrestling with food, body image, or shame, please hear me: You are not alone. You are not broken beyond repair. And you are already loved.

You do not have to shrink to be seen. You do not have to earn the love of a God Who already calls you His. No one loves like a true and living God, even in the midst of eating disorders.

Eating disorders don't just affect young girls. They silently affect women of all ages. In fact, research shows that nearly one in ten Americans will experience an eating disorder in their lifetime, with some of the highest mortality rates among mental illnesses.[1]

As this journey continues for me, I understand that this is not just a health issue. It's a spiritual battle for identity. The enemy doesn't want you to know how loved you are by Almighty God. He doesn't want you to know how precious you are to the One Who created you, and he'll do everything in his power to keep you from knowing it. But you are a precious daughter of the Great I Am, a princess in the kingdom of God. And by His grace, strength, and sufficiency, we can win this battle together.

For me, being successful in God's eyes starts with surrender. And surrender leads to peace, the kind of peace that Jesus bequeathed to us. In both surrender and peace, we find strength. And all of this ultimately leads to walking in the freedom that Jesus died to give us as He hung upon the cross.

These days, I still wake up hearing one line over and over: "The joy of the Lord is your strength" (Nehemiah 8:10).

It is more than a verse to me; it's a daily reminder. I do not have to be perfect. I just have to be present. And with God's help, I am healing, one sunrise at a time. God is doing a new thing each day.

> Isaiah 43:1 (ESV)
> But now thus says the Lord, he who created you, O Jacob, he who formed you, O Israel: "Fear not, for I have redeemed you; I have called you by name, you are mine."

DR. ROSEMARY LAMBERT-FALLS, MD, is a retired hematologist oncologist, who practiced for over thirty-five years in West Columbia, SC. She is joyfully married to her lifelong best friend, Stan Price, and they travel around the globe. When they are in the country, they spend time in South Carolina. Rosemary has touched so many lives. She is a philanthropist. She is also a heart-centered leader who loves the Lord.

Connect with Rosemary at rlambertfalls@me.com

---

1. https://anad.org/.

TRUST

Chapter 23

From "Let Them" to "Let Him"

Let them.

I never knew two words could be so powerful until I said and believed them. How could a book not found on the inspirational Christian genre shelves make such an impact on my life?

"Trust in the Lord with all your heart, and do not lean on your own understanding" (Proverbs 3:5 ESV).

God used the book, *The Let Them Theory* by Mel Robbins, to open my eyes to what He had been trying to show me. Since I was a child, I have struggled with being a people pleaser. It started with pleasing my teachers, then my friends, especially the popular kids. It worsened as I grew older. What will people think? That question seemed to preface every decision. For some reason, I valued the opinion of others, even those whom I barely knew.

I not only cared about what others thought about me, but I also got caught up in allowing them to treat me badly and accept their bad behavior towards me as my fault. After reading *The Let Them Theory,* I began to see things in a different light. "How precious to me are your thoughts, O God!" (Psalm 139:17 ESV). It was what *God* thought of me and my serving Him that mattered. This was a huge revelation. I wrote in my journal:

Let them not like me.

Let them believe what they want about me and say what they want about me.

Let them leave me out of being invited.

Let them not return my phone call or text message.

Let them rant, rave, and complain about something they think I should have done or not done.

Let them try gaslighting me.

Let them disagree with me.

For so many years, I carried the weight of anxiety over what people might have been thinking about me. I was exhausted trying to figure out why I felt such a need to be liked, accepted, and cared about.

When actress Sally Field accepted her Academy Award and told the audience, "You like me. You *really* like me," I knew how she felt. We all have our relational weak spots. Now, you know mine. Ironically, for nineteen years, I've written an opinion column for my local newspaper. Most of the feedback I receive is positive, but occasionally I am stung by criticism. Ouch! And so, a gut-wrenching incident made me realize that I had a toxic need to please others. Something was said that hurt me to the tenderest part of my heart, causing me many sleepless nights and more than a few tears. I knew I needed to figure out the intricacies of my need to please and be liked by everyone.

The person who said the hurtful words barely knew me. He wanted to believe what he thought was true. It wasn't. He refused to listen to my explanation. I was deemed guilty in the court of his opinion.

Some of you will not understand because you've never lived with this anxiety. Others are saying, "I so get this."

It was in the late fall of 2024 when I saw an advertisement to preorder a book written by Mel Robbins. *The Let Them Theory* was scheduled for release in January 2025. I read the description, quickly ordered it, and waited. I had never heard of the Let Them Theory, but it sounded like something I needed to read and ponder over.

When it arrived on my doorstep, I could not have fathomed I would be opening such a treasure chest of words my heart needed to embrace. For three days, I sat in my reading chair, holding tightly to a highlighter. By the end of the third day, I closed the book and discarded the worn-out highlighter.

Though the highlighter was dry, my eyes were wet with tears. My heart felt like it had been wrung out like a washcloth. The anxiety, from which I had suffered, had a remedy. I no longer felt like I was being held hostage by the opinions and actions of others. I knew it would take effort on my part to embrace this new way of thinking. God had nudged me to order the book. I obeyed the nudge.

Mel Robins understood my issues with people pleasing. God used a woman's words, which did not come from a Christian perspective, yet helped me see biblical truths. As I turned each page, I felt as if I were sitting in a therapist's office. My eyes read the words, but my heart felt them.

For so long, I had allowed others' opinions to control me. I made so many decisions after asking, "What will people think?"

I gave away my power like Oprah Winfrey gave away cars at Christmas: "You get some power, and you get some power. Now, will you like me?"

I also gave away my peace of mind. I allowed my decisions to flow through a sieve of other people's opinions. It was both confusing and exhausting.

I now realize I cannot control what anyone thinks about me. The thing is, they have not walked in my shoes, nor do they have any idea what my journey has been like. They view my life through foggy goggles and distorted appearances. Their vision of me is not 20/20.

Off go the chains of the opinions of others. I'm no longer a slave to what others think I should be doing.

I've been throwing away every hoop I've been handed to jump through.

I no longer wait for others' opinions to validate my decisions.

I seek the wisdom of Scripture and pray. "Let the words of my mouth and the meditation of my heart be acceptable in your sight, O Lord, my rock and my redeemer" (Psalm 19:14 ESV).

But there is more to the theory. Next, there is the Let Me aspect. I cannot control people or their thoughts about me. I have to take responsibility for my life, relationships, and connections that are right for me. This is where peace is found.

When I say, "Let me," I am taking responsibility for what I do next. I will have difficult conversations. I will not waste my time debating insignificant issues.

I will be kind and considerate of others' feelings, but not at the expense of my peace.

The *Let Me* theory does not change how I treat others; it changes how I treat myself.

“Search me, O God, and know my heart! Try me and know my thoughts!” (Psalm 139:23 ESV).

God knows my thoughts and the reasons for my actions and decisions. I pray and stay sensitive to His nudges. Obeying the nudge to order Mel Robbins’ book has been life changing.

The cover of Mel Robbins’ book says, “a life-changing tool that millions of people can’t stop talking about.” I don’t know about millions, but I do know about one. That one is me. If people disagree with my thoughts or decisions, that is on them. I’m no longer a slave to the opinion of others. I find myself calmer and more content. I’m not constantly having to explain my decisions or my thoughts unless I feel it is necessary. I’ve even been known to walk away from someone who is waiting for an argument. My silence brings the discussion to a close. I might add that this really feels good at times. I also have the thought that God is saying, “Atta girl, Janet, you are finally understanding what I want you to know.”

The book, *The Let Them Theory*, won’t be found on the shelves of Christian inspiration, but I’m so thankful I obeyed God’s nudge and ordered it. God certainly does work in strange and mysterious ways ... if we obey Him, or in other words, Let Him.

Philippians 4:7 (ESV)
And the peace of God, which surpasses all understanding, will guard your hearts and your minds in Christ Jesus.

JANET HART LEONARD is an award-winning columnist, author, and speaker who brings Scripture to life with humor, heart, and a gift for storytelling. Known for her wit and whimsical wisdom, she encourages women to believe that God isn't done with their story. He's crafting a Greatest Hits Album, not a one-hit wonder. Janet's messages, rooted in grace and real-life experience, invite others to find joy even in unfair seasons.

She's the author of *When the Hart Speaks* and is currently working on *Vintage Wisdom: Things I Wish I Knew Before I Got Old*. Book number three, a fiction title set in 1989 Kentucky, is in the works. Janet's weekly column *From the Hart* appears in *The Hamilton County Reporter*.

Connect with Janet on her website at janethartleonard.com.

CHAPTER 24

Little Miss Independent Meets Her Match

I USED TO THINK of myself as "Little Miss Independent." You know the type. The girl who declares, "I've got this!" Even when she clearly doesn't. The one who refused help carrying a mountain of grocery bags to prove a point. The woman who tried to juggle a dozen responsibilities as if she were auditioning for the circus.

That was me. I wore independence like a badge of honor. Success, in my mind, meant doing it all, doing it well, and doing it without needing anyone else's help. After all, wasn't I supposed to be capable, resourceful, and strong? People applauded those traits, and I loved the applause. Who doesn't?

The dictionary defines success as "the accomplishment of an aim or purpose." Well, if that is true, I should have been at the top of the success ladder. I climbed and climbed, convinced that reaching higher meant I was doing better. On the outside, it looked admirable. Inside, however, something more subtle was happening. I was learning to link my worth to how well I performed. As long as I kept all the plates spinning, I felt valuable. And honestly? I was convinced God was just as impressed as everyone else.

For years, as a daughter, wife, and mother, I poured myself into caring for those I loved, seeing that all their needs and wants were met. My "success" became tied to how well I cared for them. And slowly, without realizing it, I equated my worth with how well I performed even in my home.

Then life unraveled. And my carefully constructed armor cracked. It was as though God whispered into my heart, *You're not the Savior here, I am.*

Ouch. But true.

I had spent years in that sacred but exhausting space of caregiving, first walking with my dad through the fog of Alzheimer's, watching pieces of the man I knew slowly slip away. Then later, I held my husband's hand through the cruel reality of brain cancer, navigating surgeries, treatments, and the quiet moments of fear we didn't always have words for. Caring for them was both an honor and a heartbreak, and for a long time, I believed my success was measured by how well I kept everything together. Caring for others is holy work, but it cannot define our worth.

Because when the ones we care for are gone, when the applause stops and the spotlight goes dark, what then?

That was the day Little Miss Independent met her match.

I believed that if I worked hard enough, loved deeply enough, and planned carefully enough, I could keep people safe and things under control. During these tragic medical diagnoses, I discovered just how desperate I was to hold it all together. The more I clung to control, the more out of control I felt. And the more out of control I felt, the more I realized—control had never really been mine to begin with.

Scripture became my lifeline. Verses like 2 Corinthians 12:9 (NIV), "My grace is sufficient for you, for my power is made perfect in weakness," reminded me that my weakness wasn't the end of my story; it was the beginning of His strength shining through. When my armor, the shell I had carefully crafted to prove my worth, cracked wide open, I discovered a deeper peace, one that came not from striving but from surrendering.

Taking Jesus' invitation in Matthew 11:28–29 (NLT), "Come to me, all you who are weary and carry heavy burdens, and I will give you rest. Take my yoke upon you. Let me teach you, because I am humble and gentle at heart, and you will find rest for your souls," I began to learn how to rest in His strength.

The world says success is achievement, applause, or awards. For me, it used to mean being the best caregiver, the most reliable friend, or the one who always shows up.

But God's definition is different. Success in His eyes isn't about what I can hold together, but about Whom I cling to.

I began to see that success in His eyes meant allowing Him to be the Savior rather than trying to take on that role myself.

This shift didn't happen overnight. Old habits of striving run deep. But each time I found myself trying to control, I remembered, "Miss Independent has met her match."

God wasn't asking me to abandon responsibility, but He was inviting me to abandon self-reliance. There's a difference. True dependence on Him meant I could love and serve others without losing myself in the process. It meant caring deeply while remembering my worth wasn't tied to how well I performed.

It meant trading my fragile armor for His unshakable presence.

Looking back now, I see how God reshaped my story. I went from being Little Miss Independent to codependent on those around me, and finally to a God-dependent woman who understands that strength isn't about holding it all together, it's about leaning on the One Who holds me.

If I could turn back the clock and talk to my younger self, the one carrying grocery bags like they were Olympic weights, I'd say:

"Sweet girl, you don't have to prove anything. You don't have to do everything. You don't even have to have it all together. The Lord is your strength, your helper, your comforter. Let Him be enough."

Maybe you see yourself in my story. Perhaps you've worn the armor of performance or independence, trying to hold it all together, convinced that success means never dropping the ball. Friend, hear this: Your identity is not in your achievements or applause. Your identity is in Christ.

When your armor cracks, don't be afraid. Sometimes it's in the breaking that His light shines through brighter, and sometimes surrender is the bravest thing you can do.

So, if you find yourself weary and at the end of your rope today, let go. Little Miss Independent may have met her match, but in that match, she found her Maker. And that, my friend, is the sweetest success of all.

Psalm 55:22 (NLT)

Give your burdens to the Lord, and he will take care of you.
He will not permit the godly to slip and fall.

JACKIE FREEMAN is a storyteller at heart who finds healing and purpose through words. After the profound loss of her husband and parents, writing became a way to process grief and embrace a new chapter with hope. Jackie is the author of several books that inspire both children and adults. *I'm Okay, Momma!* gently introduces young readers to the fruit of the Spirit, while *Bend Your Knees, Louise!* uses the sport of pickleball to spark joy and movement. Her devotionals, including *Unwrapping Christmas* and *Keep a Song in Your Heart*, blend Scripture, reflection, and music to uplift the soul. Her latest release, *Pickleball Parables*, brings faith-filled encouragement both on and off the court. Whether through stories, speaking, or playlists, Jackie's mission is clear: to uplift, encourage, and share God's joy.

Connect with Jackie on her website at JackieFreemanAuthor.com.

CHAPTER 25

The Next Step

I SAT DOWN AT my computer to quickly update the "Books" page of my website. I added the graphic to display the Selah Silver Award for *Strength in the Storm*. Then, I noticed a statement that indicated I needed to make a critical update to my website. A warning popped up informing me I should back up my website as some things could be lost through this update. It's embarrassing to admit I didn't know how to back up my website. I ignored the warning and clicked the update button. That warning tried to tell me what *could* happen, but I just didn't think that was possible. After all, the little bots running in the invisible background should keep things in place, right?

For the next two days, I sat with tears in my eyes as I tried to fix all of the crazy things that happened on each page of my website. Pictures and graphics disappeared, and the formatting of every page was distorted. I went back and forth between two tech companies to seek help for all the components that had gone awry. I would fix one thing, and something else would be annoyingly altered when I clicked save. It was a technological nightmare. I was in such a hurry a couple of days before that I skipped the important step that could have saved my website from disaster.

As I was unloading on my husband all the stress that had ensued, he asked, "Do you need this website? How many people are you even tracking through your website?"

I had no idea. I thought, "How did I even get here?" His questions led me to fervent prayers and contemplation about what I would do next.

Have you ever asked God a question, afraid the response would be the opposite of what you were hoping? With a little hesitation, I asked Him if I needed my website. Sometimes God doesn't answer me immediately. But this time He did. He gave me a firm but gentle *no*. I went a step further and asked Him if I needed to send a monthly newsletter to my subscribers. Again, His response was no. He reminded me of the ministry call on my life: to speak life, love, purpose, and hope into the hearts of women, and that I just needed to continue to minister to the women He puts in my path and in my ladies' Facebook group that He helped me create in 2021.

I had spent three and a half years diving into training and networking to be a professional speaker for Christian women's events. I experienced the most professional growth of my life while forming kindred friendships with women speakers throughout the country. What I realized when God simply told me no was that I was building a platform based on the tried and true steps the majority of women follow to launch into their speaking career. Every ounce of training and every friendship made was worth it, but God showed me that my journey to share His goodness and to speak life, love, purpose, and hope into the hearts of women did not need to look like everyone else's. Instead of seeking Him for the next step before building those platforms, I simply did what I thought I had to do to be a successful speaker.

Just a few days before the website debacle, God spoke to me one morning while walking through my neighborhood. I was talking to Him about my future and how He wants me to serve Him, my family, and others. I knew later that day I would be having a tough conversation and disappointing someone by saying no to a great professional opportunity that God had let me know was not what I needed.

I closed my left eye and looked down at the pavement. I could see my shadow perfectly. For someone with normal vision, that's no big deal. But for me, it was nothing short of a miracle. I can barely see out of my right eye due to radiation treatment for a cancerous tumor (ocular melanoma) found and treated in my right eye in 2018, coupled with various complications since multiple surgeries and procedures.

When I saw my silhouette on the pavement, my heart leapt for joy! God has given me numerous dreams that my vision will one day be completely restored. He gave me a glorious glimpse, not just supernaturally that morning, but in the natural, of what the restoration of my vision will look like. I started jubilantly praising Him, and He spoke to me in His sweet, tender voice these precious words: *Focus on the step right in front of you*. In that moment, not only did He confirm that I was to say no to that enticing opportunity, but He let me know I only needed to focus on that moment in that day, the next step, the step right in front of me. I was so excited that I snapped a photo of my shoe in my shadow so I would never forget that moment.

As I reflected on the word God gave me that splendid June morning, I realized there are many times in my life when God has shown me to focus on the step right in front of me. During the 2008–09 school year, God opened the door for me to create a comprehensive school counseling program for students in fourth through sixth grades in a brand new rural school in northeastern North Carolina. It was my dream job.

I built great relationships with students, faculty, and families, and as the end of the school year rolled around, I was looking forward to expanding my program in the upcoming school year. But then a letter arrived in my mailbox over Memorial Day weekend, a letter I never thought I would receive. Due to huge budget cuts and a reduction in force, my school counseling position was eliminated. Just like that, everything I had built and the relationships I had formed ended abruptly. The Lord carried me through the grief, and each day, in the midst of uncertainty, I focused on His guidance for the next step.

He helped me secure a new school counseling position at a high school in a neighboring county. Before I even applied for the new job, my husband and I decided we would trust the Lord and try to get pregnant, as we knew He had perfect timing. I started the new job in mid-August, and on Labor Day weekend, I discovered I was pregnant!

When my sweet baby girl was born in the spring of 2010, I had high hopes of being a "perfect mom." Breastfeeding was highly favored in the medical community, and I knew that would be the best nourishment for her. The first few days of breastfeeding were tough, but I was determined to make it work. She was fussy, but aren't all newborns?

My husband and I took her to the doctor for her first checkup five days after she was born. A nurse checked her vitals, and a young pediatrician came into the room with a grave look on his face. My daughter had lost nearly a pound. He immediately ordered us to take her to a pediatric emergency room about an hour away. We had no idea what was wrong, and terrified doesn't adequately explain the fear we felt. We prayed, rallied our family and close friends to pray, and knew ultimately God was in control.

Prayer is the only reason I didn't have a nervous breakdown. It didn't take long to figure out I wasn't able to breastfeed, as my milk never came in. Satan tried to attack my mind that I was a complete failure, but God ever so gently let me know I only needed to focus on the next step. I learned how to feed her formula, and she thrived. I left that hospital knowing God had my daughter and me in His hands and that I only needed to focus on the step right in front of me to be a good mom, not a "perfect mom."

Just like God has walked with me one step at a time through a journey with ocular melanoma, I knew He would be with me in the fall of 2024 when I had an unrelated, two-part female surgery to improve my quality of life. Isn't it fun when gravity takes effect as we age? The surgery went well, but days later, I ended up in the emergency room with piercing pain in my abdomen, the kind of pain that takes your breath, stops every thought, and demands every ounce of your attention. After getting the pain and nausea under control, the ER doctors determined I had a large amount of air remaining in my entire mid-section from the laparoscopic surgery.

I went home a few hours later feeling so much better, but a few days later, the agonizing pain returned to the point I couldn't eat or sleep, and my body began to shake uncontrollably. My husband took me back to the ER, and this time I could barely walk on my own as he parked the car. The Lord gave me the strength to take the next step. I was hoping for immediate pain relief like my first ER visit, but this time the potent pain medication barely took the edge off.

In the wee hours of the morning before Thanksgiving, I discovered I needed emergency surgery for my severely twisted colon, a condition that could have taken my life. The only thing I could do in those dark, scary moments of pain was talk to Jesus. He showed me when I needed to get medical help, and I knew I simply had to trust Him for the step right in front of me. In this case, getting well was all I could focus on, which is quite a challenge for someone like me who is always focused on the future. I want to know yesterday what is going to happen tomorrow. This experience is a beautiful reminder to be grateful for every day He gives us on this earth and not take for granted all He provides for us to get through every day: His grace, His mercy, His love, and His healing power that touches our bodies and minds.

Let's revisit the website disaster that occurred in June of 2025. For a brief time, I honestly felt lost. How was I supposed to continue as a speaker without a website or email subscribers? When God saw my pity party needed to shift to a humbling reality, He revealed to me I had never asked Him if I needed those platforms for my ministry. Furthermore, He showed me He didn't need either platform to open the doors that He will open for me to fulfill my calling.

As the summer went on, He opened a door (and one I certainly didn't see coming) for me to start a business I had once dreamed about before my family moved to Virginia eight years prior. This new venture is out of my comfort zone, and I am trusting Him for each next step.

As I was searching for website domain names for my new business, I came across the words "next step" and I knew they had to be part of my business name because of how I help high school students and families with the college admissions planning process. I didn't even think about the vision and word He gave me earlier in the summer until I was talking with a dear friend on the phone. When I told her my business name, the Lord whispered in my heart, *Remember in June when I told you to focus on the step right in front of you?* The word He gave me earlier in the summer became part of my new business name without me even realizing it!

Psalm 37:23 (NLT) says, "The Lord directs the steps of the godly. He delights in every detail of their lives." Being successful in His eyes means trusting Him every day as you focus on the next step in your walk with Him as He helps you navigate *everything* in your life. It also means understanding that your path to fulfill God's calling on your life doesn't have to look like everyone else's. Just trust Him with all your heart (Proverbs 3:5) and He will do exceedingly abundantly above all that you ask or think (Ephesians 3:20).

Proverbs 3:5–6 (NKJV)

Trust in the Lord with all your heart, And lean not on your own understanding; In all your ways acknowledge Him, And He shall direct your paths.

SUZANNE STINES is a best-selling author and speaker who demonstrates how to have a deeper walk with Jesus when your world turns upside down. Her seven-year journey with ocular melanoma, which she shares in the Selah Silver Award-winning anthology, *Strength in the Storm: Real Stories. Real Women. Real Faith.*, has become an open door to encourage women with honest, faith-filled stories before and after the diagnosis. When you meet her, you'll find her with an iced coffee in hand, ready to hear your story and pray with you. Suzanne resides in Virginia with her husband and teen daughter.

Connect with Suzanne at home.base.with.suz@gmail.com.

Chapter 26

Sunflowers and Surrender

I LAY PROSTRATE ON the living room floor, sobbing as I begged God to lead the way. An email from a board member was still open on my laptop screen, each word like a punch to the gut as I read, "I am stepping down." I couldn't take the heaviness of life anymore. I recently resigned from a job to pursue my calling, and this news ended my nonprofit before it even started.

Sunflowers of Hope was officially a nonprofit ministry acknowledged by the state government. I was excited about the ministry God had put on my heart. It was special to me because, as a teenager, I struggled with negative thoughts and suicidal inclinations; my son struggles with depression, and my daughter has anxiety.

It wasn't until I became an adult and started following Jesus that I was able to overcome the consistent torture of those thoughts. Knowing that I could make an impact on teenagers' lives by providing a safe haven for them to better understand themselves and their struggles brought me great joy. With my board members beside me, I was ready to shine a light on mental health. We had a plan, and the future looked promising.

Instead, with each word I read, it felt as if I was in a chokehold. I began to question God and His plan. Why, God? Why now? This doesn't make sense. How could I tell my husband what just happened? What would others think of me? I felt embarrassed and foolish. What was I going to do?

As the stream of tears slowed, God reminded me this wasn't the first time I had lain on the floor crying. Two years prior, I walked away from teaching and coaching, but not before I played tug of war with God. I would resign like He wanted, but I wanted to control how and when it happened. Being the gentleman that He is, He allowed me to struggle.

In the summer of 2022, I agreed to focus more on my writing and share what God put on my heart, but under one condition. I would leave coaching, but I didn't have to leave teaching. I prayed and asked God to change my husband's heart about me not coaching. I expected God to be my "genie in a bottle." If I did what every good Christian should do, He would make my wish come true.

During this time of wishful praying, my blood pressure was high, and at one point, I was on three different medicines just to keep it in the normal range. Every four to six weeks, I was back at the doctor's office so they could check my bloodwork and try to determine what was going on with my body.

I made it through a tough volleyball season. I was not liked by a few of the parents, and that stressed me out, along with teaching seventh-grade English to some of the toughest and roughest students in that grade. I was constantly on high alert, always fearing the hammer would drop and I'd be called into the principal's office for one reason or another. Basketball season rolled around, and life didn't get any easier. By December, my husband agreed that I didn't need to coach any longer.

God answered my prayer, but we were concerned about my blood pressure. It was still out of control, and we couldn't figure out what was going on. I was doing everything they suggested, from exercising to eating a low-sodium, low-sugar, no caffeine diet. The tug of war continued between me and God while my husband and I continued to seek God's will for my future and answers for my health.

I officially resigned from teaching in April. My health slowly started to improve. When May rolled around, my heart broke as I packed up my classroom. I loved my job and my students. I didn't really want to leave, but I knew this was the best thing for me. My body couldn't handle the stress that I felt from the state, district, parents, and myself to perform at such a high standard. Like most teachers, I took my stress from work home, and I didn't take the time to relax.

A tidal wave of anxiety pulled me under as I realized I didn't know what the future would hold for me and my family. How were we going to pay all our bills and keep doing all the things we like to do? The lack of control sent me into a tailspin. There were days I didn't want to get up, but most days I went to the extreme of following a strict schedule. It was the only thing I could control.

One morning before the sweltering heat set in, I was so shaken by my routine not going as planned for multiple days in a row that I lay on the cool concrete on my back porch and cried out to God. Rivers pouring down my cheeks, I choked out, "Why can't I get a job? Why won't the days go as planned? What are we going to do? You know we can't afford this lifestyle anymore."

I was angry with God. I was hurt that He would want me to lose everything my husband and I worked so hard for. We might possibly lose all our material things because of me. What if we had to file for bankruptcy?

What if we couldn't buy groceries? I was stuck on the what-ifs and couldn't swim out of the thoughts in my head. I no longer felt successful. The seed of doubt and failure had taken root in my heart and in my mind.

As I lay there, the weight of my desires crashed down on me like a heavy blanket, suffocating my spirit. I recognized that my need to control every aspect of my life was not only exhausting but also robbing me of the peace and joy I longed for. Each moment I clung to my plans was another moment I kept God at arm's length, unwilling to fully embrace the freedom He offered.

God answered my prayer, and I was hired for a nonprofit ministry called Mercy Ships. I started working for them in July. I had one month to enjoy the summer, or so I thought, and one month to adjust to my new work schedule before Nick and our daughter went back to school.

God had different plans. He used the month of June to start breaking me of my incessant need to control everything. This change was only the beginning of learning to let go of control and to trust God with every detail of my life.

My old routines faded like the setting of the sun, and with a new job came new routines. I slowly started to realize I really wasn't in control. As my stress level went down, so did my blood pressure. My health started to improve, and by the end of the summer, I was only taking two blood pressure medications. I continued to seek the Lord and His will for my life. I studied His Word with a renewed thirst for His wisdom. Life was getting better, but here I was again, two years later, realizing I still had control issues.

I had made a huge mess of things with Sunflowers of Hope. I was heading in the wrong direction, and God had to stop me before I made it worse.

Once again, God wanted me to recognize my need for control, accept it, and release it to Him.

In full surrender, I asked God to forgive me for not seeking His will for His ministry and gave it all back to Him. God extended His grace to me that day. He met me in the middle of my mess and calmed my anxious heart. His peace was like a warm embrace from a long-lost friend. As I lay my burdens down, He whispered softly, "My child, don't you see I love you, no matter the mess you are currently in." I got up from the floor with a new sense of freedom because once again I surrendered, and God was back in control.

Our mess doesn't take away God's love for us, and it doesn't define us. When we accept that we are His, no matter how big a mess we make of our lives, and we surrender to His will, we are successful in His eyes. We will have peace, and we will be able to extend that peace like a river to those around us.

God wants to help clean up our mess. He wants to meet us in our mess so we can know Him more. I am here today sharing my story of no blood pressure medicine, a body that is functioning better than it was two years ago, and a mind made new, all because I surrendered control to Jesus. I still have days when I struggle with wanting to control every detail, but I now laugh when things don't go as I planned and thank God for changing my plans. I have learned that when God has control, I have the freedom to live intentionally and with a purpose. My life is full of joy, and for me, that is all the success I need.

I challenge you to invite God to sit with you in your mess. Take your burdens, concerns, doubts, fears, heartbreaks, and trials and lay them at Jesus' feet. Call out to God in prayer and tell Him how you feel. He will meet you in your mess. He will sit beside you, and when you're ready, He will help clean up the mess.

> Matthew 11:28–30 (NIV)
> Come to me, all you who are weary and burdened, and I will give you rest. Take my yoke upon you and learn from me, for I am gentle and humble in heart, and you will find rest for your souls. For my yoke is easy and my burden is light.

KIM HARDY is an inspiring author, Bible teacher, mental health life coach, and speaker who has overcome negative thoughts and suicidal inclinations through Scripture. In her book, *Fighting My Battles with God on My Side*, she candidly shares her struggles while encouraging readers to seek God's strength in their own challenges. This book has opened doors for Kim to bring hope to women facing anxiety, depression, people-pleasing, and perfectionism. Kim greets you with a genuine smile and loves to connect, whether on a walk or over a cup of coffee. Kim resides in East Texas with her husband, and they have two young adult children.

Connect with Kim at KimHardy@sunflowersofhope.com.

CHAPTER 27

Fragments, Faith, and a Future

THE DAY I SIGNED the divorce papers in April 2003, it felt like a funeral. Not of a person, but of a dream, a version of myself I had held onto tightly. Nine years of marriage. Two beautiful daughters, Elizabeth and Rebekah, looking to me for strength that I did not always have.

I had zero understanding of how I would make it through this challenge. I found myself a single parent in the military, away from family and friends, depleted. There I was in the courtroom alone, going through one of the most challenging times of my life, a tearing away of my heart and family by the stroke of a pen. Tears flooded my eyes. Questions flooded my mind. How would I be able to do all that I needed to do? My heart raced.

To the world, I looked put together, strong, poised, and commanding. After all, I was a military officer providing instructions to soldiers and commanding rooms with precision. To my children, I was "Mom," their anchor in a storm. For them, I wanted to ensure life would move along smoothly and be normal. To myself? I was barely standing, wondering if this was a bad dream that I would awake from soon. In a single day, my status changed from married (what I thought was a lifelong commitment) to divorced. It brought me to my knees in what felt like undefendable defeat. I felt broken and betrayed to the core of my being. My heart was shattered.Underneath the discipline of military life and the polished exterior of leadership, I began quietly breaking. I fought two wars—one in the field, and one in the home. One required strategy. The other demanded surrender. I continued to work and serve in excellence, yet one day it became too much. I realized this divorce was not a misunderstanding; it was a complete tearing away, a major shift that affected my work and family units.

I found myself single with two children to raise, who missed seeing their daddy at home. I was exhausted emotionally, spiritually, financially, and mentally. But something holy was beginning to stir. It just did not feel that way in the moment.

Be still. Be still. Yes, to be still was what I needed, yet if I did not keep going, who would care for the two lives that did not ask for this fragmented family unit? I had so much rushing through my mind. How would I afford school costs? How would I pay all the bills myself? How would I be able to handle all the responsibilities of parenting when they were once shared? Overwhelm tried to trap me. But God. Something deep inside me echoed that all things were working together for my good. And I had to pay attention to the still quiet voice inside of me. I was reminded that I was not alone. The truth was, I needed a shift to happen. The journey of letting go of the pain within would take time, for me and for my children. This was all new to us now. Life stops for no one. A Scripture from a woman's Bible study kept ringing in my soul each time I was in my closet on my knees. "And we know that in all things God works for the good of those who love him, who have been called according to his purpose" (Romans 8:28 NIV).

This verse powerfully reminds me that God is the One Who works all things for our good and His glory. All means *all*; that is all "all" means. That is it. That is all. I believe it with my heart and soul.

I did not heal through closure. I healed through Christ. God met me in the closet, not the courtroom (although even there God was present). God also met me in the car, not only in the church pew. When I had no strength left to pray loud prayers, God Himself reached me. I discovered that prayer is not reserved for the perfect. It is a lifeline for the humble. God was not looking for polished prayers. I had nothing but my broken heart to give Him. God was looking for a willing sanctuary. I—broken, tired, unsure—became His dwelling place. God showed me that He is not just building temples made of brick and mortar. He is building women of prayer who become walking sanctuaries. Every closet cry. Every whispered, "Help me, God." Every time I showed up, even when I felt hollow, those were prayers too. I found some insightful truths in the book of Isaiah. "Let no foreigner who is bound to the Lord say, 'The Lord will surely exclude me from His people.' ... For my house will be called a house of prayer for all nations" (Isaiah 56:3, 7 NIV).

Historically, according to the Bible, for centuries, worship was restricted to the "clean," the socially acceptable, the religiously elite. But here was God, flinging the doors wide open.

Everyone who holds fast to God's covenant, regardless of their background, is welcomed, cherished, and included. That includes the single mom, the divorced woman, the trauma survivor, the one with the painful past, the woman still healing. No one is disqualified from God's presence who places their trust in Him. Never forget to pray. You are His sanctuary.

God showed me I did not need to hide my humanity behind rank. My vulnerability became the bridge between me and those I was called to lead. My soldiers didn't need invincibility. They needed a leader with empathy and grace.

God Himself sustained me through the covenant of His presence. I allowed the people in my workplace to know that I was experiencing something very challenging. However, I was still committed to showing up in excellence, laced with a whole lot of grace. To my delight, there was support from that moment on. I did not need to hide my humanity. I was free to step away in moments of dire need to simply breathe when things got heavy. The mission never suffered nor lacked excellence in execution. I had hope for a better future.

My daughters did not need perfection. They needed a present mother who knew how to rise again. They were worth a mom who would walk by faith and not fear. I needed God's faithfulness. I led from my scars, not in spite of them. I became the living evidence that God could work even divorce, disappointment, and disillusionment together for good. He is the only One Who could do it.

I did not just survive. I evolved. I became a walking sanctuary. Those moments in the car, in church, and in my closet were not wasted. Something was forged in the depths of my time, calling on the source of all that I needed, my Abba Father. I became who I am today.

I am a woman of prayer. A woman who carries presence. A woman who believes that God's family is wider than tradition, deeper than trauma, and stronger than shame. If you are reading this, wondering if your story is over, let me tell you what I have learned along the way: No matter what you have been through or may be currently navigating through, you are not disqualified. You are not alone. You are not forgotten. You are certainly not finished. There is life after loss. There is power after pain. There is purpose in the fragments. This type of exchange can only occur by God's costly grace. And that? That is success God's way. Trusting Him and obeying Him no matter what it looks like, feels like, or sounds like. God is still attentive. God hears the voice of His children.

Your story does not end in survival. It begins with surrender. If this chapter spoke to you, if you are ready to lead from the fragments, then it is time to rebuild with grace.

> Ephesians 2:4–5 (ESV)
> But God, being rich in mercy, because of the great love with which he loved us, even when we were dead in our trespasses, made us alive together with Christ—by grace you have been saved.

DR. LAWANDA JOSEPH HOLLIMAN is a retired U.S. Army Colonel, transformational speaker, and author known for her signature message: *Make High Performance the Norm™*. As founder and CEO of Design High Performance™, she equips leaders to evolve, not just recover, after life-altering moments. With over twenty-six years of military leadership, a doctorate in organizational leadership, and a heart for humanity's transformation, Dr. Holliman merges strategy with surrender. She is a mother, mentor, and visionary who teaches others how to lead from their scars and live as walking sanctuaries.

Connect with Dr. Holliman on her website at
DesignHighPerformance.com.

CHAPTER 28

The Girl Who Had It All ... Wrong

As I PORED OVER the well-worn pages of my *Cosmopolitan* magazine, I said aloud, "Jill, you're really going to be somebody someday." I was an average Canadian teenager with not-so-average ambitions. The ideal for girls growing up in the 1980s was a far cry from the previous generations. We no longer had this single stream of consciousness to get married and settle down.

We were led by society to dream big in a world that was waiting for us. New role models emerged on screen, like Mary Tyler Moore, Sally Field, and Sigourney Weaver. Women were becoming CEOs, pilots, and political powerhouses. We were being suddenly *seen* for what seemed like the first time by the powers-that-be—seen as strong and independent—and I was all in.

But first, I had to somehow find my way out of the tiny town where I spent the first twenty years of my life. We had barely a hundred towns-folk, and everyone knew everybody's name. It was like purgatory to a young girl, and I was determined to escape "nowheresville." I spent hours daydreaming and plotting how this scrawny, dishwater blonde girl with bad teeth would transform and emerge from her cocoon.

After high school, I took a year off to spread my wings a little. I dabbled in live music, having been gifted musically. After that, I ran a retail clothing business and did a stint in contract work for a big-name conglomerate. I tried on different hats to see which fit. I had personality, and I could pick up new skills quickly. Finally, I found my niche: computer technology. This was *the* booming industry in the early 1990s. My first job in tech was with a company that was doing project work for the Canadian military. A spin-off of our product would be popularly known as email. Go figure.

The company was bursting with opportunity and life. This was the perfect place for me to learn the ropes. Tenacious and hardworking, I jumped from receptionist to sales assistant to partner account manager, all in the span of three years.

During this whirlwind, I found myself beginning to question the meaning of life. I was raised in church and was always fascinated by the concept of faith, but when I read the Bible, I got very little out of it. It just seemed like a bunch of folktales that didn't have any apparent cohesiveness or flow. Still, I searched. I read sermons and talked to believers from all walks of life.

In the end, I finally gave up my hard-hearted excuses and surrendered my life to Christ. I was twenty-one and on fire for Jesus. The combination that nudged me over the edge? It came down to acknowledging my imperfection, combined with a fervent hope that Jesus would come through in all the ways He claimed. And He did not disappoint.

I've experienced the love and faithfulness of God in big, bold ways. He's been there all the days of my life. The thing is, though, I have not always joined Him in the dance. I've slipped away and stumbled in profound ways. If I could name what I've struggled with most in my faith walk, it would be *humility.* Scripture states, "For all those who exalt themselves will be humbled, and those who humble themselves will be exalted" (Luke 14:11 NIV). The enemy loves to use pride as a weapon. It started with a girl in a garden in Genesis 3, and he's been creating havoc ever since.

While I was drinking from the firehose, learning the ups and downs of account management, I met my future husband. We were both teetering on the edge of thirty when we tied the knot. Brian was a good guy, funny and quirky. He could get me rolling on the floor laughing, and I put a high value on that. We spent seventeen years together and brought two adorable daughters into this world.

In the end, there were deep-seated issues that we couldn't reconcile. Had we been equally yoked and gone for some extensive counseling, who knows? Maybe we could have made it. I have no ill will toward him. We did the best we could, and our girls are the joy of our lives.

Fast-forward to the age of fifty-five. A typical day for me was rising at 5:30 a.m. to be at the gym for a five-mile run and strength training. I'd sit down by 7:00 a.m. at the computer, unless I was traveling. I hit the road about six or seven times a year. Each day, I answered an average of fifty to seventy-five emails, hopped on five plus Zoom meetings, and looked for time to troubleshoot issues and follow up on endless projects. My days were a blur. If I had stopped long enough to consider the pace at which I was moving, I would have been a little concerned. However, I was enjoying every late night, working overtime because I had a plan. Attain that next accolade. Land that next promotion. Achievement was the name of the game. Gain more, regardless of the cost to my friends, family, and my relationship with God.

Isn't it true that when we are living by a spiritual thread, life lessons can come at a terrible cost? At fifty-five, a tangle of anger and bitterness took up residence in my heart. Here I was, more than half my life was over, and I poured my life into my career. Unfortunately, I was looking at the difficult prospect of working another fifteen to twenty years to retirement.

I lost interest in men because something had turned most of them into middle-aged complainers. They seemed mainly frustrated and angry, and needed more of a psychologist than a mate. In the end, I acquiesced to dating, hoping to find a man who was at least comfortable financially. If he had some emotional intelligence, that would be a bonus.

I met John, and at first, I was attracted to him. He had everything I thought I needed. He was educated, well-off, and well-traveled. Soon enough, though, the veneer wore thin. He became petulant, domineering, controlling, and neurotic. Even with all this at play, I told myself I was happy and did my best to appear content. I settled down to a life that looked good on the outside. A good Facebook life. All show and no substance.

And then September 22, 2020, happened. I was working from home (we were all in Covid lockdown), grabbing a Coke from the fridge. Suddenly, it was as if someone just pulled my plug from the wall socket, and the entire right side of my body went limp. All the energy flowing to my right side just shut down. I recall thinking, "Hmmm, this is probably bad. Feels so permanent." Then, "I must look like a macabre sort of ragdoll." And then I slipped into a coma for three days.

It turns out that I had a hemorrhagic stroke. Only thirteen percent of strokes are hemorrhagic, and the death rate is alarming. Only half of survivors make it through the first thirty days. A quarter of those go on to live past five years. I left the rehab facility seven weeks later, unable to walk. I had complete paralysis on my right side. My daughters brought me home in a wheelchair in November 2020. Thank the Lord I stood up from that wheelchair that very first day home. I vowed never to get in that chair again. And I didn't.

Truth be told, before the stroke, I lived for fifty-five years with barely a paper cut. I had never been seriously ill. Even after years and thousands of hours of physical, occupational, and speech therapy, while I was definitely better, I had to face one unalterable truth: I would live with disability for the rest of my life.

After three years, it finally just broke me, heart and soul. I was buried in disillusionment, and I thought the story of my life was over. I felt like God had delivered me a crushing blow because, try as I may to get better, here I was, still paralyzed. The "got it all together" Jill persona that I fought so hard to regain? She didn't have a shell to hide behind anymore. My physical handicaps showed for all to see, betraying a truth we all desperately want to hide behind and camouflage. The truth is, we are all broken on the inside.

I wasn't talking to God much anymore. I was stone-cold angry with Him and was buried so deep in sadness that I didn't even know how to talk to Him anymore. Then one night in February 2024, I hit my lowest point. I got down on the floor of my apartment and solemnly asked God to show me how to live like this. I thought I was going to consider other ways of dealing with my situation. It was *that* bad. And literally, in a flash, God showed up.

In the Scriptures, God is likened to water, fire, and clouds. I felt him suddenly like a whirling wind in my mind's eye. Like a movie reel, He played back the highlights of my life in snapshots. The highs and the lows, colors and sights. Sounds and even smells. It was surreal to watch myself depicted in a memory reel. Then He slowed things down and revealed in startling technicolor what my life was like just before my stroke. It had become something that I wasn't proud of, and neither was He. I was valuing money above Him and clinging to an unhealthy relationship.

Most prominently of all, I'd become an imitation of myself. A walking billboard that said, "Check this lady out! She really has it all." Boy, was I dead wrong.

God did not cause my stroke. Bad things happen as a result of living on a broken planet. Interestingly, while His heart was broken by what the stroke meant for me, He didn't choose to address that at this staggering moment in time. My core issue, the one that was keeping me from joy in His presence, wasn't my disability. It was pride. Pride, bitterness, and resentment clogged my spiritual arteries.

He loved me enough to look past my physical affliction for now, to enter into and reveal my heart. Only the lover of my soul could stand out on that ledge with me and call me into account. And I cried what seemed like an ocean of tears. Tears acknowledging the error of my ways—surging, gut-wrenching sobs that matched the ocean of my sorrows. But there was also exquisite joy. I was wrung out utterly, so that I could be refilled and restored into right relationship with my God. How? "But if we confess our sins to him, he is faithful and just to forgive us our sins and to cleanse us from all wickedness" (1 John 1:9 NLT).

When the Lord came to my rescue that night, it was like the light came flooding back into my life. My body was still broken, but my spirit felt supernaturally whole. All the years of bitterness at not having the kind of success that I once deemed so essential suddenly disappeared into the realization that I was truly successful *in His eyes.*

I acted the very next day after this divine interruption, and I've never looked back. I ended my two-and-a-half-year relationship. I got connected to church. I started journaling (taught myself to use my left hand) and writing devotions. Now I facilitate a Bible study, and it is a blessing beyond my imaginings. I'm learning things daily, like how one soul that reaches out to know more about her Creator is worth more than any amount of wealth or status. Writing is a blessing that's now turning into a devotional book. Since that night, my heart's expanded a thousandfold. I never dreamt I would think or say this, but had it not been for my stroke, I would not have the opportunities I do.

I used to walk to the beat of the culture, adopting the world's view of success. With God's grace, I now walk to the beat of my Father's heart. I don't have wealth or status, but what I have puts both to shame: His word that I am safe and loved all the way into eternity.

> Psalm 73: 25–26 (NIV)
> Whom have I in heaven but You? And the earth holds nothing I desire besides you. My flesh and my heart may fail, but God is the strength of my heart and my portion forever.

JILL BESSE is passionate about encouraging women and helping them experience victory in Christ. God's Word has been close to her heart for nearly forty years, and at age fifty-five, she survived a hemorrhagic stroke that nearly ended her life. Out of that trial, God birthed a calling: to minister to women—especially those living with disabilities—equipping and empowering them to walk faithfully and victoriously.

Jill has served in ministry at Saddleback Church in California and now resides in Scottsdale, Arizona, where she leads Bible studies, speaks, blogs, and is currently writing a devotional book. She is honored to be a contributor to *Successful in His Eyes: Real Stories. Real Women. Real Faith.*

Her life motto can be summed up simply: "Love God, drink coffee, read books."

Connect with Jill on her website at jillbesse.com.

CHAPTER 29

When the Fixer Can't Fix

I SETTLED INTO THE chair in the doctor's office waiting room, surrounded by cheerful décor and warm light. I had never met this doctor, but I knew he was a Christian, and I felt confident he would have answers to the decade-long question I'd been asking: "What is wrong with me?"

What followed seemed to unfold in slow motion, like a two-minute emotional roller coaster packed into three short sentences.

"I have great news!" he announced with surprising enthusiasm.

Relief washed over me, and my body relaxed. "Oh, thank goodness. There's nothing wrong with me," I thought.

"You are very sick!" he added with the same tone of good news and confidence.

The look on my face must have matched the disturbing reaction in my thoughts and the tension gripping my body. *What? What did he say? How is that great news?* I considered punching him, but then the voices in my head started their familiar chorus. The condemning voice: "Now, Joni, is that how a good Christian who teaches others how to delight in God's Word should react?" The voice of doubt: "That's it. I knew it wouldn't work. I'm never going to be healthy again." Thankfully, the voice of reason jumped in: "Wait, just let him finish."

"But you can fix this," he concluded.

Those four words hit me like a physical blow. *You can fix this.*

Sitting in that sunny office, I felt my chest tighten. "God, no! Why did he say that? Why did You allow him to use those words?" I tried to push those thoughts aside and listen to the medical details: My liver had essentially stopped working, enzymes were 700 times the normal range, inflammation threatened my heart, and years of sustained stress made me a possible stroke risk.

For over a decade, I was the woman who fixed everything. I was a gold-medal-plate spinner with a successful career, a growing family, and a church leadership position. I even helped to support our fourth-generation family farm. I was the problem solver, the gap filler, the one who stepped in when things fell apart. I could quickly assess any situation and determine what was needed, then proceed to provide the solution or find the answer.

Being strong, in control, or the fixer is not necessarily a bad thing; many women live this way, operating within their genuine strengths. If you are like me, you learned to fill in the gaps of your own weaknesses and those of people around you. I operated as the fixer of all problems because I genuinely had the strength to see the big strategic picture and work towards solutions. I held all the plates spinning because I believed that was what strength looked like, what success meant.

Until I couldn't anymore.

The breaking point came when adversity piled up beyond what any human soul could balance. My family was hurting in ways I couldn't heal. How was I going to fix the unethical practices in my workplace? How could I recover physically from surgery to correct years of chronic pain? Who was going to save our family farm from decades of debt from previous generations? How could I live without the one person whose love I'd never questioned? When was I going to stop feeling bitterness and anger every time I looked at my husband? How would I be honest about my lies and mistakes and dig myself out of the shame and guilt of a failing business?

Worst of all, my beautiful daughter was being beaten and abused by a husband she desperately wanted to love and change. How could I protect her and my precious grandson from evil in their own home?

These were the questions that haunted me for over a decade as I slowly slid into a lonely pit of disappointment, discouragement, and the deepest despair of depression. I lived in a spiritually weary, emotionally fatigued, and hopeless mental state. My hope was replaced with apathy and numbness. The fear was overwhelming and paralyzing, leading me to make reckless and foolish decisions that complicated my life into unrecognizable disorder.

All my plates crashed to the floor, shattering into ceramic dust. I didn't have the strength to fix any of it anymore. But God. He came to rescue me, heal me, and use me to help others do the same.

I'd spent three years climbing out of that pit—confessing, surrendering, trusting, often starting over again. God faithfully restored my hope, teaching me that I didn’t have to be the fixer of all problems. I didn't need to provide every solution or always be strong. He was the Fixer. He was enough.

My first book, which shared this very testimony of God’s faithfulness and healing, was released the week of this doctor's appointment. This was supposed to be a time for celebration, for sharing how God had worked in my life to restore hope. Instead, I was gripped with fear that I had to fix something *again*.

"You can fix this."

The words were paralyzing. I couldn't go back to being the fixer. I would never make it out of that pit again. How could I still be sick when I'd healed so much emotionally and spiritually?

Once I was safe in my car, I picked up the conversation with God. He had some explaining to do. "I am not the fixer. I am tired of fixing and healing. Why did he say it? I don't have it in me. This was supposed to be the time I started thriving." I cried and yelled out loud. Still in the parking lot, my phone rang. It was my husband. Something snapped inside me, and I answered with confidence and a cheerful hello.

"What did the doctor say?" he asked.

Before I could think about my response, my mind went into default mode—one I thought I had eliminated. The habit of being strong and in control. The fixer. "The doctor found some concerns in my blood work, but said I could easily make some changes to fix it," I replied. There was no sense in getting into the details on the phone, but honestly, it allowed me to decide how and what I would tell my husband and my kids. I didn't expect the news I received or to spend the next year fighting a new battle of healing and fixing.

When my daughter called later, I broke down in tears. "I can't do this again. I can't be the one who has to fix everything."

"Mom," she said gently, "let's figure out what this looks like and make a plan. You can do this. God isn't done writing your testimony, and you know He's faithful. So, what's the problem?"

She was right. The problem was that healing doesn't always have a one-time fix. This was just another layer. Healing often requires us to continue the journey with perseverance and hope, revealing new areas to address. I *could* do this, not because I was the fixer, but because I'd learned who my true strength was.

During those months of recovery, God brought Moses to my attention repeatedly. Studies, dreams, random sermons—Moses everywhere. I could almost hear Jan Brady shouting "Marsha! Marsha! Marsha!" but mine was "Moses! Moses! Moses!" At first, I wondered why. Then I understood.

Moses had weaknesses. He couldn't speak well, he struggled with doubt, and he got angry. But God called him anyway. God didn't remove Moses' shortcomings; He promised to be with him. God didn't ask Moses to fix the Egyptian situation. He asked Moses to trust in His presence while *God* did the fixing.

God revealed His character as faithful, merciful, holy, and patient. God showed Moses how to rest in God's sufficiency, not his own strength. Even when Moses wrestled with insecurity, anger, and doubt, God did not leave him.

The God of Moses became real to me in new ways. He equipped me with everything I needed, including a supportive family. I adhered to a balanced diet plan and received guidance from medical professionals. But more than that, He reminded me of what I'd learned in my healing journey: I participate in the process, but I'm not responsible for the outcome.

This wasn't about being strong enough or capable enough. This was about obedience. It was about showing up day after day, following the plan, trusting God's faithfulness even when I felt weak. God was saying, "I will be with you," not "You're on your own to fix this."

The God of Moses is the God Who equips me. He doesn't ask me to abandon responsibility, but He invites me to abandon self-reliance. He's the God Who has healed and shaped me over time, through weakness and strength, and remains faithful even when I struggle. He is the Fixer and Perfecter of my faith.

Success in God's eyes isn't about being the woman who never breaks, never needs help, never has problems. It's not about fixing everything or having all the answers.

Success in His eyes looks like Moses—flawed, weak, uncertain, but willing to trust God's presence. It looks like showing up imperfectly but faithfully. It looks like doing the next right thing, even when you can't see the whole staircase. It looks like resting in God's sufficiency rather than striving in our own strength.

The world says success means having it all together, being the one with solutions, never showing weakness. But success is letting Him be God while I allow myself to be His beloved daughter, equipped, supported, and never alone.

My liver numbers returned to normal within a year. I still have to fight for my health and manage my stress, but the true Healer is with me every step of the way. The same God Who met Moses on the mountain met me in my doctor's office and in my healing journey. Just like He was with Moses. Just like He is with you.

Exodus 3:12 (NIV)
And God said, "I will be with you."

JONI ROSEBROCK is a Bible teacher, speaker, and author passionate about helping women overcome lies with the truth of God's Word. Through her signature framework, *WRAP Yourself in the Word™* (Write, Read, Apply, Pray), she equips women to build lasting faith habits and live with confidence and freedom in Christ. Joni leads coaching groups, creates Scripture-based tools, and hosts the *WRAP Yourself in the Word* podcast. She is known for her kind yet witty teaching style, which makes biblical truths practical for everyday life. When she's not writing or teaching, you can find her enjoying quiet moments on her family's Ohio farm with her husband, Randy.

Connect with Joni on her website at jonirosebrock.com.

Chapter 30

Audience of One

I REMEMBER SITTING IN the audience at a MOPS (Mothers of Preschoolers) convention as the lady stood on stage and started speaking. I don't remember her name or what she taught that day, but I do remember vividly thinking, "I could do that. God, I would really love to be able to encourage other women in their faith and their calling. But I want to do it with the right motives. I want to do it for You and Your glory, not mine, because I will mess it up and be miserable."

I went home and continued to be a stay-at-home mom for the next fifteen to eighteen years. I dreamed of being a writer or a speaker, as podcasts were not a thing back then, but the business of being a mom took priority. I started a blog for a little while, but I wasn't consistent, and it faded away into the archives of Blogspot.

I began to think the dream was just my ego, and with each passing year, it seemed less and less likely, like a chalk picture smudged until it's almost unrecognizable. After all, there were lots of other women writing and speaking, and they had kids, so I thought there probably wasn't anything special I had to say. Smudge. And I couldn't seem to make the time or get over my fears, so there must be something wrong with me. Big smudge.

The picture grew fuzzier and fuzzier until I started believing God must have something else for me.

Don't get me wrong, I loved being a mom. I always wanted to be a mom, and I feel motherhood is a high calling. It is also undervalued in the world, and I struggled at times with feeling like I was "just a stay-at-home mom."

The time came when my youngest went off to college, and I started thinking about what I wanted to do now that the kids were grown. I was sad they were not at home, but I was getting excited about the new possibilities. I could finally do all those things that I had been putting off. One morning I was cleaning the kitchen when my husband called. I could hear the stress in his voice. The woman who had been running the radio station for him had found a wonderful opportunity elsewhere, and she was leaving in three weeks. There was not enough time to find, hire, and train a replacement. He needed me to come in immediately and help.

I wasn't exactly thrilled to be dragged back into the radio station full-time because I saw it as an interruption to my plans. I now see how God used it to get me pointed in His direction.

After I had worked a few weeks at the radio station, my husband, knowing my dream to write and speak, approached me and suggested I take a thirty-minute time slot available on Sunday morning. I could play contemporary Christian music and share some thoughts and inspiration in between. I would love to tell you I jumped at the chance and ran with it, but I hesitated. Years of wanting with nothing happening had taken its toll. Proverbs 13:12 (NIV) says, "Hope deferred makes the heart sick," and I was filled with insecurity and doubt.

My stomach did a few flip-flops, and not the fun ones you wear to the beach. Could I really do this? Would I have time? Would it be any good? Would anyone really listen to what I had to say? Fear was fighting against hope and threatening to smear my dream into oblivion. I learned many years ago that when you pray and seek God, He will give you a sense of peace about the answer, even if you are shaking in your boots. The rest of the verse is, "But a longing fulfilled is a tree of life."

I said yes and started doing the show. The dream of writing and speaking began to take shape again, and I had a new life. Have you ever felt a dream you thought was long dead stirring back to life? After overcoming the initial fear and a lot of editing, I was producing a regular Sunday morning show.

As the next two years went on, I got the hang of my show, and about the time I was getting comfortable, I felt that internal niggle that God wanted me to take it up another notch. I started speaking and studying a little more, and then had the idea of having a conversation with a friend. A spark went off! I enjoyed having conversations so much more than talking to the microphone by myself. I wanted to have more conversations, and then I knew I wanted more people to be able to hear these great conversations on more than just Sunday morning, so the next step was a podcast.

I am not a tech-savvy person, so the thought of learning everything needed for a podcast was very intimidating. Almost paralyzing. After lots of tears and fears (a nod to some of the music we play on our station), I finally got everything in place and launched the podcast.

It was exciting that people could now listen on more than just Sunday morning, and I could see how many people were listening. With radio, one never really knows how many people are listening, but there is data with podcasts. Well, the excitement soon turned to disappointment, because the numbers on the podcast were not impressive. The numbers were embarrassingly pathetic, like single-digit pathetic. But I kept going.

Zechariah 4:10 (NLT) says, "Do not despise these small beginnings, for the Lord rejoices to see the work begin." I had a few people say they listened, and some of my guests said I did a good job, so I was encouraged for a while.

In the back of my mind, though, was an expectation that if I did a good job, the podcast would be successful. Like in the movie *Field of Dreams*, "If you build it, they will come." I had good content with amazing people and inspiring stories, but success in the podcasting world is numbers and rankings. I had neither.

I was spending a lot of time and resources to host the podcast, find guests, read books, and record and edit the conversations. Not to mention the promotion side of websites, emails, and platform building on social media. For those of you who enjoy social media, God bless you. For some of us, it is more fun to break out in hives than think about content creation and scheduling consistent posts. All this work for results that didn't measure up. Was it worth it?

I hope I'm not the only one to have gripe sessions with God. Some of my gripe sessions went like this: "Why aren't you moving, Lord? I've been working hard to do a good job, and I'm not seeing results. I believe you called me into this, and I am getting discouraged. What is wrong with me? Am I doing something wrong? Do you want me to move on to something else?"

People kept telling me to be patient and persistent, but shouldn't I see some sort of result by now? I know Galatians 6:9 (NIV) says, "Let us not become weary in doing good, for at the proper time we will reap a harvest if we do not give up." But just how long before there is a harvest?

One day, I received an email at work. I was sitting at my desk at the start of my workday and saw a forwarded email from the station website. It was a listener who wanted to have a copy of the transcript of the show I did on hope. Oh! This was flattering. I sat up a little taller in my seat and kept reading. She wanted to be able to read it to her husband because it brought him hope and encouragement. Aww! That is so sweet. He was dying of heart disease. What? The screen went fuzzy from the tears that sprang up in my eyes.

Suddenly, the numbers didn't matter. Something I did on my show brought hope and comfort to a dying husband and his wife. And it wasn't even a conversation; it was my voice that God was using. (There is another lesson in the value of everyone's voice, but that's for another day.)

There is a popular story by Loren Eiseley of a little boy walking along the beach. The sandy shore is covered in starfish. One by one, he picks them up and throws them back into the water. A man walking along the beach says to the boy that he can't make much of a difference because there are too many starfish for him to save them all. The boy replies, "I made a difference to that one!"

When I first told God that I wanted to encourage other women through writing and speaking, I also prayed that I would do it with the right motives. I believe God knew if I had impressive numbers with thousands or millions of downloads right away, I may have lost sight of the true success in obedience and perseverance. Colossians 3:23–24 (NIV) says, "Whatever you do, work at it with all your heart, as working for the Lord, not for human masters, since you know that you will receive an inheritance from the Lord as a reward. It is the Lord Christ you are serving."

I was getting discouraged because I didn't seem to be making much of a difference, but I was measuring by the world's standards. When I remember that I'm working for an audience of One, the Lord, I'm encouraged to be obedient and perseverant in the purpose He has for me, to use my gifts for His glory.

That is where success comes from, not numbers. We can get so easily caught up in the world's definition of success: the titles we have, the money we make, the awards we receive. And yet none of them last. The most important reward is "Well done, good and faithful servant" at the end of my life.

I am called to do my job to the best of my ability and then leave the results to God. Just because I may not look as successful as someone else with impressive numbers on a podcast, or numerous followers on social media, or a massive amount of money in the bank, I am still successful in God's eyes.

No matter what my numbers look like or how many awards I have on my wall, God says I'm chosen (1 Peter 2:9, Ephesians 1:4), loved (John 3:16), forgiven (Psalms 103:12), precious, and honored in His sight (Isaiah 43:4). He rejoices over me with singing (Zephaniah 3:17).

When we are obedient and persistent in what God has called us to do, no matter how big or small the task, we are successful in His eyes.

Matthew 25:21 (NIV)

His master replied, “Well done, good and faithful servant! You have been faithful with a few things; I will put you in charge of many things. Come and share your master’s happiness!”

LISA GRANGER is an award-winning radio host, podcaster, writer, and speaker, who is passionate about reminding women that their voice, story, and dreams matter. With ten years in radio—conducting hundreds of interviews and earning multiple VAB awards—plus over 120 podcast episodes of *A Woman's Heart with Lisa Granger* and contributions to *God is Faithful: 30 Days. 30 Women. 30 Stories. One God*, Lisa creates space for authentic conversations sprinkled with humor. A "recovering supermom," she knows the freedom found in Christ and loves encouraging women to pursue the passion God has placed in their hearts. Lisa lives in Virginia with her husband, adult kids, and dogs, and enjoys coffee, dark chocolate, music, travel, sassy shoes, and laughter with friends.

Connect with Lisa on her website at lisagranger.com.

Chapter 31

Miles, Files, and Hymns

My parents ran freight with the dedication and endurance of marathon runners. They maintained a steady pace and focused on the next mile marker. A phone always remained glued to their ears, and receipts spilled out from the visor. They built a trucking brokerage from a hotel room desk and a Rolodex.

When Mom wasn't helping Daddy book loads and get clients, she was the closing manager at a real estate firm. Binder clips, payoff letters, and calendars so full they begged for mercy covered the passenger seat of her car. She moved between lenders and title companies, shepherding files across the finish line.

They were successful at what they did. And they were always on the go, which paid for cheerleading camp and kept the lights on. I was grateful for that, but it was also a constant reminder that there was no room in their passenger seats. They didn't have time for me.

But God knew. God, in His mercy, gave me Bertha. My parents hired her as a nanny and housekeeper, and she became my miracle. Bertha showed up when my childhood felt overshadowed by my parents' ambition.

Even in their absence, my parents loved me. Mom kept my macaroni art in a file marked "Personal—Do Not Purge." Daddy carried my school photo in the pocket with his rate sheet. The kitchen calendar looked like a dispatch board. If the day was highlighted yellow, Mom had closings; pink meant she was on the road. If the day was blue, Daddy was out booking loads with better margins. But Bertha filled in the rest with home cooking, church songs, tough love, and the laughter so deep I can still feel it.

Though my family did not attend church, Bertha brought church to me.

Bertha turned our house into a home. With her, our home felt comforting, like a little small-town clapboard sanctuary filled with song. And oh, my goodness, Bertha could sing! She cooked to "Great Is Thy Faithfulness," ironed to "Blessed Assurance," and scrubbed to "Nothing but the Blood." At bedtime, she'd put her hand on my forehead and sing "Leaning on the Everlasting Arms" until fear let go. "Baby," she'd whisper, lifting her gaze toward heaven, "don't waste none of it." By "it," she meant everything: scraps in the skillet, minutes before bedtime, heartache with tears that could water tomorrow's flowers.

She lived church out loud every day. She prayed over the kitchen sink, and she shared life lessons between spelling words and cheer practice. She would sing "Trust and Obey," and my smart mouth would soften. "But God!" she'd say, and then she would share some inspirational story. My soul would feel renewed, as if I had taken a breath of fresh air. She taught me to love Jesus as if He were sitting at our table, asking for seconds. She taught me that obedience is love with feet on it. That the pressure in life, just like an olive press, is where the oil runs, and when life puts its weight on you, you say yes to Jesus and watch what He squeezes out: mercy, patience, and songs you didn't know you knew.

As I grew older, memories of Bertha's living-room faith held me steady; hymns at the sink became my bedrock, especially during challenging times.

Over time, we noticed that Daddy began to forget. He misplaced his keys. And the man who had spent a lifetime with a photographic recall of maps suddenly struggled to find his way home from the grocery store. Then he began forgetting his words and how the kitchen drawers worked. We followed him down a long hallway named Alzheimer's, turning off lights as we went.

He was still my daddy—handsome, stubborn—and he loved to dance. Even as names fell away like fall leaves, his rhythm stayed. I could put on Garth Brooks or the Temptations, and his feet would remember what his mind could not. When confusion fogged the floor, I'd hum "Amazing Grace," and he found the "how sweet the sound" part every time. We slow danced in the living room, and when the song ended, he'd whisper, "My sweet little girl," as if the past was a window he could still see through for a second.

Mom's body turned into a weather map of pain. Autoimmune storms rolled in without permission. Every day was different, and the forecast was always wrong. Some mornings her joints screamed like a fire alarm; some nights her skin felt like a bruise no one could see. The woman who once wrangled lenders and agents into harmony now measured distance in steps from the bedroom to the chair. Mom had been an expert at being busy, but she never learned to be still.

The day came when "We got this" became "We need help," not just for rides to appointments or occasional casseroles, but for my husband and me to move countries, move them in with us, and provide full-time care. It was a *big* ask: to make a home for those who hadn't been there for me. I stood looking out the window of our flat and felt the old ledger book crack open, all the frustration and resentment bubbling up. In the middle of my "This is too much" and my "It's not fair," I heard Bertha's words: "Don't waste none of it. Use what I poured into you." Obedience, again.

So, we moved back to the United States from Germany and bought a homestead in the hill country of central Texas, big enough for all of us, with a wide porch, long table, and rooms that could hold our history without buckling. Caregiving became my new role. I learned my dad's medicine schedule the way he had learned rate charts. I labeled drawers with pictures. I made a playlist of oldies on Spotify to dance to, and we glided in socks on the hardwood. When he asked for his mother, who had been gone since I was in high school, I took his hands and said, "She loves you, and so do I." When he couldn't find my name, I answered to "sweetheart" or "Hey, you" because love knows it's loved even when misnamed.

I managed Mom's care with the attention to detail she had used when closing files, drawing on the lessons of love and faith that Bertha instilled in me. Days were filled with pill boxes, heating pads, rheumatology appointments, and the alphabet soup of diagnoses that finally spelled, "We don't know why it hurts, but it does," all while I made meals that were more like hugs. I rubbed lotion into hands that once juggled HUD statements, payoff letters, and keys. We laughed at nothing until it was something. We watched court shows and *Survivor,* trying to guess who would be jailed and who would be voted off. I said, "Tell me again about the day five files funded at once." And she did, and I let the good parts be the loudest ones.

There were hard days. I paced the backyard, telling Jesus He'd have to loan me His patience before I used up mine. I cried in the laundry room because it's loud in there, and the washing machine can cover you like a choir. I remembered birthdays with babysitters and concerts where I searched the crowd for a face while she reconciled a closing package across town. The old ledger book kept trying to read itself aloud. But Grace closed it, with a gentle hand and a song. "Honor thy father and mother" stopped sounding like a chore and started sounding like choreography: step, turn, sway, breathe. Obedience is love with feet on it and a hymn in its mouth.

God did more than help me care for them; He let me carry them to Him, home-church style, Bertha-simple.

With Daddy, we'd been dancing to "In the Midnight Hour," then I switched it to "I'll Fly Away." His eyes were as clear as they ever got those last months. I said, "Daddy, do you want to fly away to Jesus, to have Him be your Lord and Savior?"

He cocked his head as if he could hear a far-off train and said, "Mmm hm."

I kept it plain, the way Bertha prayed over sink water and spelling lists. "Say, 'Jesus, forgive me, I'm Yours.'" He did, and we both cried while I softly sang the last verse. Not long after, he slipped home to Jesus between "I love you" and an old Garth Brooks song called "The Dance." We danced him to the edge; Jesus led him the rest of the way.

With Mom, the journey was longer. She believed there was a God, but she didn't know Him. She was mad at Him. She was mad that she was sick, mad that her husband died, and mad at me for not being mad. She had lost herself in the weight of chronic pain, and the only thing louder than the pain was her fears.

So I went with what I knew; I made our living room feel like a church again, with no pews (just her recliner) and no organ (just a humming fridge). We sang hymns and read Psalms in the slow voice you use with the sick and the stubborn, because she was both. One afternoon, while I was telling her about a ministry I served in, she asked, "Is it too late for me?" We prayed without fancy church words: "Jesus, forgive me. I am yours." She opened her eyes less scared than before. The pain remained, but new hope had her sitting more upright in her chair. Knowing Jesus, and two years after Daddy, she went to heaven.

After Daddy's funeral and later Mom's, we did what Bertha had taught me: We sang while we worked. I found a mason jar of drippings I kept out of habit and holiness. I made gravy that tasted like memory and mercy. My kids and grandbabies danced with me to the Temptations, then helped me wash dishes to "I'll Fly Away." I told them stories about a man who could sell you a smile and a woman who could close five files a day, about a nanny who turned a living room into a clapboard church with nothing but a wooden spoon and a song, and about a Jesus Who wastes nothing.

If you are reading this and you had parents who lived on the road or just weren't home, chasing loads and deadlines and keeping the lights on, hear me: God can rewrite that into a beautiful story, even if your memories are more highway than hugs. He poured His love into me through a singing nanny who taught me hymns at home, and then He poured it back out through me when the road ended at our door. He turned missed dinners into a feast of second chances; calendars became choreography. My "I can't" evolved into "I can do what You ask," all set to music.

Through this journey, I've learned that success is not about booking the most loads or closing the most files. Success in God's eyes looks like a small, steady yes: over the sink, in a waiting room, on a makeshift dance floor between a recliner and a record player, in a living room that doubles as a sanctuary. It's honoring the people who gave you life by bringing them to the Lord Who gives life eternal. It's doing what you can with what you have and trusting God to catch what you can't.

"She hath done what she could," Jesus said once about a woman who poured out all she had while the room called it waste. When I think of Bertha's church hymns, my parents' miles and files, my halting obedience, the moving back, the doctors, the praying, and the singing, I gave it all I had. It saved them, and it healed me, too. I am overwhelmed by the blessing that only God is big enough to put all the broken pieces of my life back together and heal all of it.

But God! He didn't waste a mile. He didn't waste a tear. He didn't waste a song. He turned road miles and closing files into home-church hymns, and He is still teaching me to trust and obey.

> Psalm 147:3 (NIV)
>
> He heals the brokenhearted and binds up their wounds.

KAREN COLLIER's faith was forged as God rescued her from an abusive marriage and complicated family situations. For more than thirty years, she has taught Bible studies and spoken at women's groups, retreats, and conferences, including to military spouses overseas. With a blend of Scripture, storytelling, and practical steps, Karen encourages women to live a steady yes with Jesus, trusting the One Who rescues, restores, and writes beauty into even the messiest seasons of life. She is also the author of the *Wandering Tails* children's series, inspired by her eight giggling grandchildren. Karen lives in Wimberley, Texas, with her husband and family.

Connect with Karen on her website at droverjacks.com.

Chapter 32

Trading Self-Reliance for God-Dependence

Tears streaming down my face, I sank to the kitchen floor in defeat. Surrounded by remnants of a Sunday breakfast gone wrong, I felt like an epic failure. My adult children were visiting for what I'd planned as the perfect family weekend with my new husband, Brian. I had choreographed every detail—game nights, hiking in the dunes, stories around the campfire—determined to prove that our blended family was Pinterest-worthy.

My husband found me there in the smoke-filled kitchen, covered in pancake flour, and scooped me into his arms, lightly kissing the top of my head. "It's going to be alright, honey." Then he calmly salvaged what remained of breakfast.

Later, as we cleaned up after the kids left, Brian said, "Honey, I don't like it when your kids come to visit."

Wait, what?

My heart plummeted. But he quickly continued, "Not because I don't like *them*, but because I don't like who *you* become when they're around.

You're critical and demanding. You get stressed out when things don't go the way you planned."

He was right. In my desperate attempt to create the perfect experience, I had become someone no one wanted to be around—least of all myself.

You'd think that would have been a turning point for me, but it wasn't until several years later that the truth in that moment finally sank in. For me, it came after a lengthy season of caregiving for my terminally ill mother. I was soul tired. Not just physically exhausted (though I was that too) but weary in the deepest parts of who I was. That's when God intervened. In May of 2021, within the span of a week, God sent three different women who didn't know each other to deliver the same message: I was a hot mess and needed to stop and rest. Not sleep rest—though I needed that too—but true soul rest. The kind that requires getting away with Him and keeping company with Him.

One woman told me to slow down. Another said I needed to stop trying to tackle everything by myself. The third encouraged me to take time to lament and spend time with Jesus. Their words broke through my stubborn self-reliance like nothing else had.

God showed me I needed to quit everything and just spend time in His presence. I cancelled commitments, stepped back from projects, and learned what Jesus meant when He said, "My yoke is easy and my burden is light" (Matthew 11:30 NIV).

During this season of forced stillness, I found myself drawn to the story of Jesus calling His first disciples. Picture these ordinary fishermen going about their daily tasks—mending nets, sorting the catch, running their family business. Suddenly, this Rabbi walks up and says two simple words: "Follow Me."

That's it. No business plan. No explanation of benefits. No time to think it over or discuss it with their family. Just an invitation that would change everything.

And here's the part that astounds me: They dropped their nets immediately and followed Him.

I used to think this was about a one-time decision, a dramatic moment of saying yes to Jesus. But as I sat in my own season of surrender, I realized the Christian faith isn't built on a single yes. It's built on a thousand small ones. Every day, Jesus extends the same invitation: "Follow Me." And every day, we choose whether we'll drop whatever we're clutching or keep holding on.

For me, the nets I clung to weren't made of rope and cork floats. They were woven from my need to control outcomes and my attachment to being seen as a woman who "has it all together." These nets felt like security, but they were actually keeping me trapped in exhaustion.

The invitation to follow isn't just about walking behind Jesus geographically. It's about releasing our white-knuckle grip on everything we think gives us identity and security. Our carefully planned schedules, our perfectly curated reputations, our five-year goals, our need to be needed. When we truly follow, we hold it all with open hands, trusting the One Who called us will provide everything we actually need.

As I surrendered my frantic pace, I discovered what the Bible has to say about working from a place of rest. Jesus modeled this perfectly. "Very early in the morning, while it was still dark, Jesus got up, left the house and went off to a solitary place, where he prayed" (Mark 1:35 NIV). And then there's Luke 5:16 (NIV): "Jesus often withdrew to lonely places and prayed."

Jesus withdrew from crowds regularly. He said no to demands and opportunities. He prioritized solitude and prayer over ministry activity. Work flowed from His connection with the Father, not the other way around.

I began to see the difference between self-reliance and God-dependence like contrasting two trees. Self-reliance produces exhaustion and burnout, like a stunted shrub in the desert (Jeremiah 17:5–8). God-dependence produces sustainable ministry where you experience peace and rest, like a tree planted by streams of water, drawing life from the Source.

I started practicing what Mary of Bethany understood: the wisdom of choosing what matters most. While her sister Martha was caught up in the whirlwind of hosting duties, Mary made a different choice. She sat at Jesus' feet and listened to His teaching (Luke 10:39).

Mary chose presence over performance. When everyone else was rushing around, she deliberately positioned herself as a student at Jesus' feet, not because there wasn't work to be done or people to serve, but because she recognized the greater opportunity and intentionally chose it.

This transformed my understanding: Jesus Himself is the treasure. Not our accomplishments for Him. Not the results we achieve. Not the recognition we receive. Simply Him. He is both the journey and the destination.

When Christ becomes our greatest treasure, letting go becomes natural—even joyful—rather than a struggle or a sacrifice. True success isn't measured by what we build or achieve, but by "the surpassing value of knowing Christ Jesus [our] Lord" (Philippians 3:8 CSB).

The life of faith centers on discovering that Christ is enough. It's accepting His invitation to "Come to Me" and learning to simply be with Him.

It means choosing to slow our pace, quiet our hearts, anchor ourselves in His truth, tune our ears to His voice, immerse ourselves in His Word, and remain connected to Him.

This is what weary hearts truly long for: the beautiful simplicity of finding everything we need in Christ. Not more formulas or success strategies, but simply accepting Jesus' invitation to come to Him. It's His call to stop performing and start being fully present—to create enough quiet space that we can actually hear His voice about the constant noise of our endless obligations.

Three years after those initial three women confronted me and my burnout, God brought my story full circle. In May 2024, He sent three more women who didn't know each other. But this time, they came with words of blessing.

Again, within a span of a week, three different women commented that the peace they saw in me was remarkable. One even said that I *exuded* peace. Imagine that! This former perfectionist and control freak now radiated peace. Only God!

I call this my "rooster story" because, like Peter's restoration after denying Christ three times, God was showing me the transformation that had taken place. While I hadn't denied *knowing* Jesus, I had denied the *power* of His Spirit by trying to do life on my own. God replaced the words of caution with words of blessing, completing the story for me.

The difference? I had learned to rest in God's presence, not in my performance.

Through this journey, I've discovered that success in God's eyes isn't about external recognition but internal transformation. It's not being driven by the desire to be seen, known, and celebrated, but by love for God and genuine concern for others.

Success in God's eyes asks, "What is God calling me to be faithful in today?"

Jesus says, "I am the vine; you are the branches. If you remain in me and I in you, you will bear much fruit; apart from me you can do nothing" (John 15:5 NIV). God's definition of success is the only one that matters.

I'm learning to remain connected to the Vine, trusting that when I abide in Him, fruit will come naturally. I'm discovering the freedom that comes from working in God's power instead of my own, measuring success by faithfulness instead of results, and prioritizing obedience over outcomes.

The invitation stands before each of us: Will we continue exhausting ourselves trying to do it all on our own? Or will we learn the beautiful rhythm of working from a place of rest in the Lord? Success God's way isn't about doing more—it's about surrendering more. And in that surrender, we discover that He really is enough.

Matthew 11:28 (NIV)

Come to me, all you who are weary and burdened, and I will give you rest.

CHRISTINE HOY is an author and speaker devoted to helping Christian women break free from the exhausting cycle of perfectionism and discover true peace in Christ. Through her book, *Peace Beyond Perfection: Overcoming the Fear of Not Being Enough*, and her REST Framework—Release, Embrace, Surrender, Transform—Christine guides women toward embracing their authentic identity in Christ rather than striving for impossible standards. She speaks at women's conferences, retreats, and church events, offering encouraging and grace-filled messages that resonate with women longing to exchange perfectionism for God's perfect peace.

Follow this link to receive Christine's gift to you:
https://christinecarterhoy.com/devotional/

Chapter 33

A Legacy of Love

It was 4:00 a.m., and my mother didn't know her phone had dialed me. As I answered, I was startled because I was unsure of what was happening on the other side of the line. Not to mention, I was over 600 miles away and helpless.

I kept saying, "Mom. Mom, are you okay? What's going on?" I heard her and my father talking as he was trying to get her to the bathroom. Her legs were beginning to wear out, and needs were now evidently beyond his caretaking capabilities. I heard them bantering back and forth, and then a loud cry from both of them as she fell to the ground. His final act of love was to call an ambulance and relinquish control to those who would take over until her ultimate death from cancer.

Since I live in North Carolina and they were in Syracuse, NY, I could not easily be a strong presence to help through these final days. I was a divorced single mother who had to work and was not in a position to stop my life to take care of my mom. Needless to say, that broke my heart, but God provided through church, family, and friends. That brought enough peace to sustain me. Yet periodically, I would ask the Lord to tell me when I needed to go home. That incident was the megaphone to drop everything and be there to say my last goodbye.

On that trip, I saw the Scriptures come to life through my mother's inevitable last days and death. The bravery she exhibited is beyond what I could ever have.

She continuously proclaimed, "I could never do this without Jesus." And she didn't.

The last months of her time here on earth were heartbreaking and enlightening at the same time.

Although cancer was more dominant in her body than healthy cells, she wholeheartedly talked about her faith and the peace that Jesus had given her.

She made it to eighty years on July 18, 2025. I made a special trip to celebrate this milestone with her. Through that week's visit, I accompanied her to her doctor's appointment and procedures. It was a bittersweet honor. It also gave a much-needed break to my father, who had been the steady rock assisting her every need for over seven years.

Her birthday celebration consisted of some friends gathering around her bedside with singing and laughter. It was all she could handle. She coughed up blood, could barely walk, and didn't eat much. She became more and more lifeless as the days wore on.

The back and forth with doctors as to possible solutions toward survival was getting more and more grim. We knew this metastatic thyroid cancer was incurable, but the unrelenting efforts of Western medicine still offered solutions, regardless of quality of life. I also knew deep down that, although my mom was ready to go be with Jesus, she was hoping for a cure.

However, she needed a voice of reason. I had to convince her, my father, children, friends, and loved ones that this is no way to live. I asked God to help me be that voice of reason. His ultimate medicine of eternal rest was all we needed going forward. I believe my mom was feeling Philippians 4:7 as the days went on. The peace that surpasses understanding is beyond our mortal cognition. But it is real, and she had it in her final months.

Here is how God was at work in those final days. Whether they wanted to hear it or not, anyone who crossed Mom's path heard about Jesus and His power through her pain. Along with handing out *Jesus Calling* devotionals like candy, she was ministering and sharing the gospel of Christ to any nurses or doctors who had ears to listen. She'd say, "Why would I still be here at eighty years old, dying. It must be to share Jesus with other people before the Lord takes me home."

My father is not a believer, yet he was a steadfast caretaker, lover, and provider for my mom during her last days. No matter how strong the pride of his ways overpowered a relationship with Christ, he was in the presence of a woman who glorified Jesus through it all. No matter how heavy his anxiety overpowered him, he witnessed her peace that surpasses understanding. The Holy Spirit was active in his home and marriage. In his wife. Could we assume that was God's plan during her last days? My dad was a witness. And God is not the God of coincidence.

Mom made her confessions of Christ to my dad often and in the presence of dozens, even hundreds of witnesses. In fact, I believe that was the main reason God kept her here on earth. Even through the suffering, sleepless nights, coughing up blood, she had a purpose to share the gospel, proclaiming God is good, even when the world isn't. God is faithful, even when you live in fear. God is the God of hope, even when your future looks bleak.

During those final days, I saw God's power through pain and purpose. After the middle-of-the-night phone incident, the next day in the hospital, my mom was frustrated over a lack of communication with one of the doctors. In that frustration, she sent me a text saying, "Jodi, I wish you were here!" Not once during this cancer journey did my mom ask me for anything, especially a trip that would have been costly, jeopardizing my loss of work and income. Since I had asked God when I needed to be at her bedside, I believe He spoke right through that plea. In obedience to God, I rushed home to be at her hospital bedside that weekend.

When I walked into her room that Sunday morning, I didn't expect to see what I did. My strong, vibrant, hardworking mother wasn't there. Instead, I saw a lifeless human barely hanging on. I couldn't seem to remember her or her energy. Her humor. Her voice. My mother was still here, breathing, but it was becoming more labored and distant. I found myself missing the mom who raised me. Provided for me. Taught me. Loved me.

She knew I was there that Sunday morning. She could still communicate and understand. Many friends and family came to visit over the days to come, knowing this was their last goodbye. The nurses and doctors would come in and out, administering end-of-life care, basically pain management. She didn't eat and only drank mere ounces. The doctors advised that this could take many days to weeks for her life to end since her heart was very healthy.

I could not imagine this woman, my mom, suffering like this. It's not fair. It's not human. It's not right.

Psalm 23:4 (NIV) spoke volumes to me during this time. "Even though I walk through the darkest valley, I will fear no evil, for you are with me; your rod and your staff, they comfort me." And it did. He did.

Back in the day, that Scripture used to be read at funerals. It never made sense to me because it really wasn't intended for death. It was intended for life. Words can't express the comfort the Lord gave me and my family during this difficult time.

We don't have to like what happens to us in life, but we have to trust God is bigger than our circumstances, and that in the midst of the devastation of cancer, He can do a work in us and the world around us.

In many ways, I could understand my mom's faithful perspective through a debilitating cancer. I pray I never experience a disease that becomes a physical and mental breakdown, but in God's economy, it's all relative and manageable under His hand. And His grace is sufficient through it all, as it was so sufficient for my mom during this battle.

Even in the wee hours of the morning, despite her inability to sleep, she still revered and glorified God during this tribulation. We would pray, and she would proclaim excitement over meeting Jesus. She was so encouraging.

What makes this anomaly of a godly life to death so profound is that I have witnessed it in real time through my own mother. It's her legacy, how she lived and died for Christ. It's what we call a "purpose-driven life." It answers the lifelong question: What on earth are we actually here for?

We read in 1 Timothy 6:12 (NIV), "Fight the good fight of the faith. Take hold of the eternal life to which you were called when you made your good confession in the presence of many witnesses."

I believe my mother did just this. I was a witness to a woman who maintained peace under the physical chains of cancer.

Mom always used to say, and I believe these words came from her earthly father, "We're not of this world; we're only in it for a very short time."

Mom and I talked about Jesus every day. Right before her death, she told me how awesome it is that we are so close, how much she loved and adored me, how we could talk about anything and always circle it back to Jesus. How many daughters and mothers have that relationship? I was weeping when she said that. It was so real. And so true. She also made it very clear that I am to let everyone know who Jesus is.

Every day from that Sunday, I saw a tremendous decline in her health. On average, each day her body failed approximately 25 percent, which was faster than the doctors' predictions that she could be here for weeks. I prayed, "Lord, take her. We are ready." And I believed she was too. Yet God's timing is perfect. It wasn't until my special needs sister made an unexpected visit on Wednesday, September 10, 2025, that God revealed his end-of-life date and time. He took her home, and she was at final rest. I believe she needed to feel Jill's presence to finally make that transition.

It's a bittersweet honor to help walk your mom home to Jesus. But through it all, the Lord made clear that success doesn't depend on what happens to us in life, but how we allow God to handle it.

We may not be able to avoid cancer, divorce, mental health struggles, or addictions. However, we can still have success in His eyes when we invite His peace in fear and His hope through doubt.

Psalm 23 isn't just a funeral Scripture; it is a living Scripture for the living world. It reminds us that the Lord is our Shepherd, and we shall not want. When life gets hard, He lies us down near beautiful pastures, beside quiet waters, and He gives us rest. He is the refresher of our souls, guiding us along the right paths, under His namesake. God anoints our heads with oil, which in return gives us a joy that allows our internal hearts to overflow with the fruit of the Spirit.

You can call my mother a warrior, and you can say she was strong, but she would have said, "I'm simply a weak daughter that serves a strong God." We have success in His eyes when we trust God, Who supernaturally infuses the ability to live through the hardest struggles in life. I can say this with honesty because I've tried doing life without Jesus Christ, and it simply didn't work.

Here is the promised reward from God. When the Lord decided to take Mom home on Wednesday, September 10, 2025, at roughly 9:00 p.m., I was able to feel the peace that surpasses understanding because of the Christ that we both knew. This season taught me that a death in Christ will be laced with peace. Though I miss her terribly, her last act on earth showed me what it meant to be ushered into the presence of our Savior, and that is ultimately the final act of success for a believer.

Philippians 4:7 (NIV)
And the peace of God, which transcends all understanding, will guard your hearts and your minds in Christ Jesus.

JODI HOWE is a worship leader, vocal coach, performer, speaker, podcaster, and author whose mission is to bring hope and encouragement through faith-filled inspiration. She is the author of *The Air That I Breathe* and a contributing author to several Christian anthologies. Whether leading worship, performing throughout her community, or mentoring vocalists, Jodi's heart for ministry shines through her authentic stories and relatable truths. She reminds others that God can transform struggles into strength and pain into purpose. When she's not serving in ministry or teaching, Jodi enjoys time at home in North Carolina with her children and her cat, finding peace in music, prayer, and quiet reflection.

Connect with Jodi on her website at jodihowe.com.

Conclusion

Do you see it now?

You are the woman with the alabaster jar.

You've been her all along, kneeling at Jesus' feet with your most precious offerings, pouring out your life while voices around you calculate the cost. Maybe those voices have been inside your own head, whispering that you're wasting your time, your talents, your one beautiful life on things that don't matter to the world.

But you've read these stories now. You've met women who chose the invisible over the impressive, who discovered that God's economy turns everything upside down. They poured out their lives like perfume, and the fragrance filled every corner of their world.

You've learned what they learned: *You are already successful in His eyes.*

Not because you've achieved enough or proven enough or become enough. But because you are His daughter, His beloved, His princess in the kingdom that will never end.

The world will keep its scorecards. Let it. You're no longer measuring yourself by standards that were never meant for you. You're free now to do what you can, with what you have, right where you are, and to know that this is enough. More than enough. It's everything.

So, what happens next?

When that voice whispers that your work doesn't matter because no one sees it, you remember that One does. When comparison tries to steal your joy, you close your eyes and hear His voice: "She has done a good and beautiful thing." When you're tempted to pursue what glitters instead of what glorifies, you pause and ask, "Whose approval am I living for?"

Here's my prayer for you, my friend: May you walk forward with the confidence of a woman who knows her worth. May you pour out your life with the abandon of one who understands that nothing given to Jesus is ever wasted. May you discover, in a thousand small moments, that faithfulness in hidden places creates a fragrance that reaches heaven.

You don't have to wait for permission to live successfully in His eyes. You already have it.

Now go, dear princess. Break open your alabaster jar. Pour out your treasures without counting the cost. Live for the audience of One Who sees you, knows you, and calls you successful simply because you are His.

The world may not understand. But He does. And His opinion is the only one that will echo into eternity.

She did what she could.

So do you.

Invitation to Review the Book

Thank you for reading *Successful in His Eyes*!

I pray that *Successful in His Eyes* has encouraged and inspired you to see yourself as God sees you—beloved, chosen, and equipped for His purpose.

If this book has blessed you, would you take a moment to leave a review on Amazon?

Your words—no matter how short—help others discover the message of hope and truth found in these pages.

Thank you for helping share God's light with others!

Made in the USA
Coppell, TX
20 February 2026

71810227R00148